The Act Of Service

Your Guide to Public Roles and Becoming Influential in the UK

Bukky Okunade

Published by Find A Fresh Publishing

ISBN 978-1-0684655-6-7
ISBN 978-1-0684655-7-4

Dedication

Dedicated to those who selflessly serve and have devoted their lives to acts of service. Your commitment and sacrifice inspire and uplift countless lives.

Table of Contents

INTRODUCTION

I began writing *The Act of Service* with great excitement. For most of my life, I have aspired to be someone who works to help others, finding fulfilment in knowing that my efforts on their behalf have resulted in positive outcomes. My dedication to serving others and my strong desire to contribute to the betterment of our society have been the driving forces in my life, both at home and in my fields of work in local government, the voluntary sector, and the community.

Everyone, in my opinion, has a distinct purpose and something valuable to offer. We all seek inner happiness, which I have discovered can be found when we use our skills to benefit others. When you feel obligated to give back to your community, whether with your money or your time and abilities, you leave a legacy that surpasses your lifetime. Therefore, your purpose is to invest some of your time in making a positive difference in the lives of others.

You can make a difference in society by getting involved in small ways, one step at a time, right where you are. You can start by addressing any issues that concern you, like I did. When my child was unfairly denied admission to a local primary school, I felt deep frustration that I couldn't ignore. I questioned the decision, challenged the process, and pushed for answers. That experience opened my eyes to the broader issues within the education system. If this could happen to my child, how many other families faced the same barriers without a voice to represent them? Even though my child later got admission, I was determined to do more than just fight my own battle; I sought ways to be part of the solution. I attended school meetings, spoke to other parents, and researched how decisions were made. That's when I learned about the role of school governors. They are the people who help shape policies, influence school leadership, and ensure accountability. It was exactly the kind of position where I could make a difference.

I put myself forward, and when appointed, I took the role seriously. I listened, learned, and, most importantly, spoke up. Whether it was advocating for fair admissions, pushing for better resources, or questioning policies that didn't serve all children equally, I made sure I used my position to drive change. That step to governance became the foundation of my journey in active service, proving that real influence starts with getting involved.

Starting an initiative, like a community or volunteer group, is also a great way to make a difference in the community and address specific difficulties. Your success depends on what you do, how committed you are to the cause, and how well you can work with influential people who may occupy positions of power. You don't have to wait until you have significant power in a position of authority to make a difference. What really matters is recognising the problem, acting, and showing that you are committed to reaching your goals. If you wonder why no one else is doing anything about an issue, ask yourself, "Can I make a positive change here?" If you have some spare time, getting involved in projects like these can help you and your community in many ways.

Co-founding the Thurrock African Group in 2003 and transforming it into an organisation running a community radio station by 2020 has been one of the most rewarding experiences of my life. During the pandemic, the station supported the Black and minority ethnic community, later becoming a platform to train young people in media and life skills, boosting their confidence and expanding their opportunities. Being able to help others has been deeply fulfilling and has continued to drive my commitment to service.

With deep respect for her legacy, Queen Elizabeth II embodied a life of unwavering service. Taking the throne at just 25, she dedicated herself fully to her nation, the Commonwealth, and its people. Her impact was profound. Her late Majesty championed charitable causes, supporting hospitals, schools, and other institutions that help those in need. She was the Patron of the Queen's Commonwealth Trust, which helps young people all over the world to make a difference in their communities. Beyond duty, she was a devoted mother and grandmother, balancing service with family. She was also known for her love of animals and her dedication to animal welfare, actively participating in several animal welfare organisations.

The Queen's life was a testament to the power of selfless service. It is a legacy that continues to inspire us all.

"When I was 21,
I pledged my life to the service of
our people and I asked for God's
help to make good that vow.
Although that vow was made in my
salad days, when I was green in
judgement, I do not regret, nor
retract, one word of it."

Queen Elizabeth II
1926-2022

People participate in acts of service in numerous meaningful ways, each contributing uniquely to their communities and the world. Some dedicate themselves to careers in medicine, caring for the sick, and saving lives. Others step into humanitarian roles, providing vital aid to those affected by conflict or disaster. Many serve in the military, dedicating themselves to the protection and defence of their country. Additionally, individuals in positions of leadership, from running nations to holding influential roles, shape policies that impact the lives of millions. Each act of service, no matter the role, plays a crucial part in creating a better world.

Reading this book, I hope, will help you realise how broad the term "act of service" is and give you some ideas for how to succeed in your own journey towards public service.

PART ONE

Understanding Service

CHAPTER 1

DEFINING ACTS OF SERVICE

The first act of service I can remember wasn't something I sought out; it was something that found me. Growing up, I was mostly focused on myself. Like many young people, I wasn't thinking too much about helping others or making a difference. But that changed when I went to boarding school in Nigeria.

It was there that I got my first real taste of service. I was appointed as a food prefect. Now, you might think that meant I was just passionate about food, but no, it wasn't about that at all. It was a role of responsibility, a role that required me to make sure every student got their fair share of food and that order was maintained in the dining hall.

Let me paint a picture for you. There was a busy dining hall filled with over 300 hungry teenage girls. Ten girls sat at each long table, eagerly waiting for their meal. Without someone to oversee the process, things could get chaotic; some would push ahead, some would take more than their portion, and others might be left without enough to eat. It was my job to bring order to the chaos, ensuring that every girl at every table received her fair share. I learnt many initial lessons from serving there, such as understanding that to achieve equality and make a meaningful impact, one must have a systematic approach and be prepared to embrace the responsibility of leadership.

WHAT IS AN ACT OF SERVICE?

An act of service is any effort, big or small, that brings help or comfort to others. Whether it's volunteering, supporting a cause you care about, or simply brightening someone's day with a kind gesture, these actions create meaningful connections and make a positive difference in the lives of those in need.

Service isn't limited to individual actions; it can happen on a larger scale. Schools, hospitals, and government bodies have the power to create lasting change within communities. Working with these institutions or even being part of them, whether through volunteering or holding public office, can enable shifts in attitudes, policies, and systems. It's how we can make our society fairer, more inclusive, and more caring.

So, whether it's a small gesture or a bigger commitment, acts of service help make the world a better place. It's something each of us can take part in, contributing in our own way to the well-being of those around us.

Why Get Involved?

At first, as a prefect in school, I didn't see it as a big deal. But over time, I realised that when you serve people well, they feel good. Something as simple as making sure meals were distributed fairly had an impact. It created order, harmony, and a strong sense of community among my peers. Looking back, I see that moment as a small but significant step in my journey of service, which would shape the rest of my life.

Taking part in acts of service can be a rewarding experience for everyone involved. It's not just beneficial for the people you assist but also for you and your community. Imagine lending a hand to someone in need, like helping an elderly neighbour with an errand such as picking up their groceries. Not only does it make their day easier, but it also brings a sense of fulfilment to you.

In fact, serving others can sometimes mean saving a life. Many years ago, there was a sad incident in my neighbourhood: a man passed away, and his body remained undiscovered for over four months, only to be found when a gas company attended to read the meter. If people had been checking on their neighbours regularly, perhaps somebody would have noticed his absence much earlier and might have even been able to give him the support that he needed.

There are many reasons to be involved in an act of service. Here are just a few examples:

Transforming Lives: By volunteering at a homeless shelter, for example, or assisting a neighbour in need, you can truly transform lives. Your time, resources, or donations become invaluable to the lives of those less privileged. The impact you can make is real, tangible, and profoundly meaningful.

Personal Growth: Service isn't just about giving; it's also about receiving. It's a powerful tool for self-improvement. With every act of service, you gain new skills, boosting your self-esteem and developing a sense of purpose. It's a journey of personal growth that never ends.

Building a Stronger Community: Acts of service can help to strengthen communities. Volunteering and community projects, such as cleaning up a local park, bring people together to work towards a common goal. When individuals from diverse backgrounds come together for a common cause, it helps bridge gaps, promote connections, and build a more resilient community capable of dealing with challenges.

Enhancing Leadership Potential: Committing to acts of service can help individuals to develop leadership skills. Volunteering and community service projects often require individuals to take on leadership roles, such as organising events or leading a team of volunteers. This can help to develop skills such as communication, delegation, and problem-solving, which can be valuable in both personal and professional contexts.

Civic Engagement: Serving others helps you become a more active and responsible citizen. It connects you to your community, keeps you informed about important issues, and encourages participation in making a difference.

Through service, you play a role in building a stronger and more engaged society.

Influence: Influence is often misunderstood. Many people associate it with power, wealth, or fame, but true influence goes beyond status or authority. To be influential is to inspire, guide, and shape the thoughts, decisions, and actions of others. It is the ability to create change, not by force, but through respect, credibility, and impact.

In the context of public service, influence is about making a difference in your community, workplace, or even on a national scale. It is about leading by example, using your skills, experiences, and values to improve lives and shape policies. Being influential does not mean holding the highest office; rather, it is about effectively contributing to society and empowering others.

In summary, carrying out acts of service is a magnificent journey of win-win scenarios. It's about improving the world while enriching your life in countless ways. So, embrace this journey, and watch as you transform not just the lives of others but also your own as you contribute to a brighter, more connected, and more compassionate world.

Key Requirements for Acts of Service

I once had a conversation with a woman of Pakistani origin who aspired to become a councillor in the UK. She was deeply passionate about her community, full of ideas for positive change, and eager to represent voices that often went unheard. But there was one thing that prevented her from even trying: it was her fear of public perception. She worried that people would judge her accent, believing that all the councillors in her area were well-spoken in a way she felt she wasn't.

"I worry that people won't take me seriously," she admitted. "What if they don't understand me? What if they judge me for the way I speak?"

I paused for a moment, then said, "The power of leadership isn't in how perfectly you speak; it's in what you have to say. Your accent is part of your story, a reflection of your journey. Don't see it as a barrier; embrace it as a strength."

I explained that having a distinct accent could be an advantage. It could make her stand out, help her connect with diverse communities, and bring a unique perspective to the role. "What you see as a limitation," I told her, "could be the very thing that sets you apart and drives you to achieve even more."

This conversation made me realise how many people hesitate to serve because they believe they lack one thing or another.

To make a real difference through acts of service, the qualities you need are a genuine desire to help, a heart full of empathy, and a vision to improve the world. So, what does it take to truly serve effectively? While the act itself is simple, a few key ingredients make it impactful.

First, be prepared to dedicate time to your cause. Service is a commitment, not a single event. It calls for devotion, which comes from a genuine belief in the good you're trying to achieve. You should feel it in your heart, like a deep-seated desire to make things better. Bring enthusiasm to everything you do. Think of it as the secret ingredient that adds energy and passion to your service, making it more impactful and inspiring to others. Integrity is also essential because service is about doing what's right, even when no one is watching.

While leadership can be a powerful asset, you don't need to be a superhero to make a positive difference. Leadership skills grow and evolve with experience, and by taking the initiative and empowering those around you, you can amplify your impact. With these qualities in hand, you're ready to make a meaningful difference through service. And the best part? Your passion will encourage others to follow your lead. Let's explore each of these qualities.

Commitment of Time

Dedicating one's time is an essential component of any act of service. In our daily lives, we all allocate a significant portion of our time to various commitments, such as family, work, and personal leisure. If you aspire to engage in community service, you must be prepared to carve out some dedicated time for it while also maintaining a healthy work-life balance in all other aspects of your life. Being available for committee meetings and staying informed by reading reports are among the numerous responsibilities that accompany the role of a council member and serving the public. Consequently, assuming significant responsibilities within a life of service demands a high level of commitment and a willingness to actively participate in activities that support a cause dear to your heart.

Devotion

Devotion is the unwavering commitment and heartfelt dedication that underpins acts of service, especially in church volunteering. It reflects a deep connection to faith and community, inspiring selfless giving of time and energy for the greater good.

Whether teaching Sunday school, uplifting spirits through worship music, or mentoring youth, volunteers embody love, compassion, and dedication. Their service strengthens bonds, nurtures spiritual growth, and creates a lasting impact, demonstrating how faith in action transforms lives.

Desire

An act of service is more than just a kind deed; it manifests the desire that motivates individuals to give back to their communities. Take the role of a school governor as an example. Their willingness to serve is rooted in a passion for education, commitment to the well-being of students, and high standards for academic achievements. The love for education and the welfare of children and young people drives school governors to serve voluntarily. Their desire to ensure quality education motivates them to oversee school policies, budgets, and curriculum. They dedicate their time to attending meetings, reviewing data, and providing valuable insights, all aiming to enhance the learning environment for students and enrich their lives for a brighter future.

Enthusiasm, Persistence, and Perseverance

Enthusiasm, persistence, and perseverance are essential qualities for acts of service, especially for those aspiring to public service. These traits define a leader's ability to connect with people and overcome obstacles.

Enthusiasm drives a public officeholder to engage with constituents, understand their concerns, and present a compelling vison for the future. A leader's energy and commitment inspires trust, motivating communities to rally behind a campaign.

Persistence ensures that dedication does not waver in the face of obstacles and setbacks. Political campaigns, for example, often encounter hurdles, challenges, and opposition. A persistent candidate stays focused, adapts to changing circumstances and works tirelessly towards their goals. Furthermore, persistence keeps initiatives alive and ensures that promises made to the public are pursued with determination.

On the other hand, perseverance is the determination to endure through trials and tribulations. It's about standing firm in adversity and maintaining integrity throughout the campaign. Perseverance helps candidates weather controversies and negative campaigns, emerging as resilient leaders ready to serve their constituents.

Together, these qualities shape leaders who win elections and lay the foundation for effective and principled governance.

Integrity

Given the general public's mistrust of authorities today, integrity is more important than ever for those in positions of trust. It's essential for effective acts of service in any capacity, from elected office to that of a non-executive director. It gives the public hope that their interests are represented fairly and honestly. Integrity is the focus of always acting in accordance with one's stated values and principles. Warren Buffett wisely noted, "In looking for people to hire, you look for three qualities: integrity, intelligence, and energy. And if they don't have the first, the other two will kill you."

Having integrity requires a dedication to truthfulness, accountability, and making ethical choices, and it goes beyond simply adhering to a code of conduct. Leaders who put ethics first earn the respect of those they serve. Leaders with integrity consistently make decisions based on the highest moral standards.

Leadership

Leadership is key to serving others effectively. Those passionate about helping others often inspire and encourage action through their vision, adaptability, and problem-solving skills. Both formal and informal leaders contribute meaningfully: formal leaders, like elected officials, step up to serve based on conviction, while informal leaders use their experience to support causes within their communities. True leadership requires courage, creativity, and consistency, as shown by figures like Mother Teresa and Nelson Mandela, whose dedication and resilience set powerful examples. While some may be natural leaders, leadership skills can also be developed to maximise one's impact.

Overcoming Challenges in Acts of Service

Making a difference through acts of service depends greatly on individuals' commitment, but several challenges can make it feel like an impossible goal. Resources and time are two of the most difficult constraints you may face. However, when you step back and look at the big picture, you'll realise that management is the only way to deal with these problems. Financial management and time management are arguably valuable skills to have. Other factors that may be holding you back include a lack of knowledge, a lack of support, distractions, procrastination, self-doubt, and a fear of what others think. Below are some common problems and strategies to overcome them.

Volunteering and Financial Concerns

Volunteering on a limited budget can be challenging, especially when expenses like travel and accommodation are involved. In some cases, charities may offer travel reimbursement, but many volunteer roles are unpaid.

To make volunteering affordable, focus on essential costs, create a budget, and explore grants or funding. Partnering with like-minded organisations can also provide support. Avoid unnecessary spending. Financial stability allows you to contribute more effectively. With smart planning, you can make a meaningful impact without straining your finances.

Finding Time

Finding time for acts of service can be challenging with busy schedules, balancing work, family, and other commitments. However, effective time management and prioritisation can make it possible.

Start by assessing your daily routine: making small adjustments can free up time for service. Breaking tasks into smaller commitments rather than tackling everything simultaneously makes it more manageable. Even a few hours each week can create a meaningful impact over time.

Consider involving family and making volunteering a shared, enriching experience. With planning and intention, making time to help others is always within reach.

Procrastination

"Procrastination is the thief of time," said Edward Young, and the truth of this statement is clear today. Delaying tasks leads to missed deadlines and opportunities, especially when pursuing personal growth or applying for important roles like non-executive positions. To succeed, discipline and prompt action are essential. The key to overcoming procrastination is self-motivation. Align your thoughts with your goals and act without delay. An accountability partner can also help by offering support and keeping you on track. Success requires focus, discipline, and timely effort.

Lack of Knowledge

Fear of not being qualified or knowledgeable can hold people back from service roles, like politics or non-executive director positions. The key to overcoming it is understanding that learning is a lifelong process, as no one starts as an expert. Personal growth often comes through service, and mentorship can help develop both skills and confidence.

Lack of Support

Pursuing a path of service, whether in public office or community work, may not always receive support from family or friends. Doubts or negativity can make you question your decision.

To address this, communicate openly about your passion, values, and the impact of your work. When others see how it benefits both themselves and the community, they may come to understand. Surround yourself with like-minded individuals who uplift and support your journey. Having a strong network can help you stay motivated.

Distractions

In our busy lives, distractions like excessive social media use can quietly consume our time, making it harder to serve our community or engage in meaningful activities. To stay focused, we must practice self-discipline, set clear boundaries, and establish realistic goals. By being mindful of how distractions creep in and prioritising what truly matters, we can remain dedicated to helping others and making a difference.

Fear of Judgement

Worrying too much about what others think can hold you back. Fear of judgement often stops people from taking action, as they worry about criticism or how their efforts will be perceived. While seeking advice is valuable, it's important to stay true to your beliefs.

Negative feedback may arise from misunderstanding or doubt. Some may say, "This won't work," or "You're not suited for that role," but it's up to you to assess if their words hold weight.

To overcome the fear of judgement, focus on why your goal matters. Not everyone will share your vision. Seek guidance when needed, but do not let opinions deter you. Stay committed, trust your purpose, and the doubts of others will carry less weight.

Self-doubt

Self-doubt can be a major obstacle for those wanting to serve, whether in local government or parliament. Uncertainty about your abilities may make you feel unqualified, preventing you from taking action. However, as Susan Jeffers writes in *Feel the Fear and Do It Anyway*, pushing past fear is key; everyone experiences anxiety in new situations.

To overcome self-doubt, focus on your strength and celebrate small wins. Positive self-talk and recognising your progress can build confidence. Seek support from those who appreciate your efforts; their encouragement can reinforce your belief in yourself. Even small acts of service create a real impact. As you see the difference you make, your confidence will grow, motivating you to keep going.

Your Well-Being While Serving

Service roles can be deeply fulfilling, but it also requires ongoing effort, which can take a toll over time. To ensure that you can continue offering support without feeling overwhelmed or burnt out, it's essential to care for yourself along the way.

In November 2023, Rt Hon Therese Coffey, a public servant in the UK who had served in high-profile roles, including Deputy Prime Minister and

Secretary of State for Environment, Food and Rural Affairs, resigned, citing work-related stress. She revealed that five years prior, she had become seriously ill due to the pressures of her ministerial duties, leading to her decision to step back from government roles.

Her resignation highlighted a reality that many people, not just public servants, experience: burnout. The pressure to serve, lead, and support others while maintaining an image of strength can be overwhelming.

Burnout occurs when someone becomes emotionally and physically exhausted from giving too much of themselves. This can happen when someone devotes too much time and energy to serving others. To avoid burnout, it is important to set boundaries and prioritise self-care. This can include taking breaks when needed, practicing mindfulness or meditation, and making time for hobbies and activities that bring you joy. It is also important to recognise when you feel overwhelmed and ask for help when needed.

Taking care of yourself is not selfish; it is essential. Prioritising your well-being ensures your service remains sustainable rather than short-lived. Whether leading, volunteering, or supporting loved ones, balance allows you to serve with energy and compassion. Let's explore how to prepare for service effectively in the next chapter. True service starts with intention, preparation, and the right mindset.

Summary of Chapter 1
Defining Acts of Service

- **What Constitutes an Act of Service**: An act of service is defined as any action, big or small, that helps, comforts, or positively impacts others, ranging from personal gestures to large-scale community efforts.
- **Benefits of Service**: Engaging in acts of service offers personal growth, strengthens communities, enhances leadership skills, fosters civic engagement, and can lead to life-changing transformations for both the giver and the recipient.
- **Key Requirements for Service**: Effective service requires commitment, devotion, enthusiasm, integrity, leadership, and a genuine desire to help, emphasising that anyone can contribute meaningfully regardless of background or resources.
- **The Ripple Effect of Service**: Every act of service has the potential to create a ripple effect, inspiring others to engage, creating a culture of giving, and driving collective progress towards a better society.
- **Overcoming Challenges**: Bukky discusses common obstacles like time constraints, self-doubt, and fear of judgement, and provides strategies such as effective time management, seeking support, and maintaining a strong sense of purpose to overcome these challenges.

Chapter 2

Preparing for a Life of Service

When I committed to standing for councillor, I didn't have every answer, but I had a clear reason for doing it. I wanted to be a dedicated champion for the community, ensuring its needs and concerns were addressed. That purpose became my anchor, keeping me focused even when the journey felt uncertain.

Of course, making an impact requires more than good intentions. Before committing to any service role, it's important to take stock of your life, your work, family, and existing responsibilities. Service is about giving, but it should never come at the expense of your well-being or stability. By preparing thoughtfully, you set yourself up for success, ensuring your contributions are meaningful and sustainable.

If you're considering a leadership role or a way to give back, start by asking yourself, what is my purpose? What do I hope to achieve? Clarity on your goals will help you find the right opportunities. Next, build your network and connect with people already serving in the roles that interest you. Learn from their experiences, seek mentorship, and find ways to get involved at a smaller scale before taking on bigger commitments. The following key steps will help you prepare for service roles:

Discover Your Purpose

Identifying your purpose is one of the most important steps in preparing for a service role. When you align your passions and values with your commitment, you become more effective and focused. Your core motivation for building a better society might originate from various experiences, including conversations with others, following current events, or engaging with media.

Take time to reflect on the causes that resonate most deeply with you. Are you passionate about healthcare, education, environmental protection, or social justice? By examining these areas, you will gain clarity on where you can have the greatest effect and focus your energy on what matters most to you. The clearer your purpose, the more meaningful and fulfilling your service will be.

Having Clear Goals

Having clear objectives serves several important purposes in your journey to serve others. It helps you identify relevant opportunities and decide where to invest your time and energy. With defined goals, you can ensure your efforts align with your greater vision, whether becoming a voice for the voiceless or addressing a prevalent social issue. Ultimately, you'll know you are headed in the right direction if you can clearly answer the question, "Why do you want to serve?" This question helps refine your purpose and solidify your determination to make a difference.

Whether you're looking to strengthen your skills, advocate for systemic change, or support a particular community, having clear goals for your acts of service is essential. When I became a school governor, one of my primary objectives was to help every child reach their full potential. Taking on the additional role of Special Educational Needs (SEN) link governor allowed me to further this aim by ensuring that all children received an inclusive education, with adequate support for those with special educational needs in mainstream schools. Clear goals gave me the focus and direction to make a lasting impact.

Networking

While having clear goals gives you direction, building a strong network provides the support and opportunities needed to bring those goals to life. Prime Minister Winston Churchill's journey to leadership wasn't solely shaped by his ambitions, but also by the people who supported him along the way, especially his mother, Jennie Jerome. She was a key figure in his life, offering both emotional support and strategic connections that helped him into the political world. Her networking, both in social circles and political realms, opened doors for Churchill at critical moments in his career.

Networking isn't just about who you know; it's about engaging with individuals who share your passion, learning from their experiences, and being open to the guidance they offer. Like Churchill, building relationships with like-minded people and organisations can inspire new ways to make an impact, provide invaluable insights, and ultimately help bring your goals to life.

Attending conferences, seminars, and workshops related to your interests can help expand your network and introduce you to fresh perspectives. Engaging in online communities, joining social media groups, and participating in discussions aligned with your goals can also lead to valuable connections. Platforms like Meetup.com and other networking sites make it easier to find and connect with people who share your commitment to service. Through these relationships, you gain new opportunities and essential support and encouragement.

Equally important is surrounding yourself with positive, supportive individuals. Connecting with those with experience in your area of interest can be immensely beneficial. Before my first election as a councillor in 2006, I had the privilege of meeting a group of female politicians who organised seminars to promote women's political participation. Their encouragement demonstrated how networking can empower individuals to support one another in their journey of service.

Using Google and Other Online Resources

Networking plays a crucial role in finding service opportunities, but in today's digital age, technology makes it even easier to discover ways to get involved. Search engines like Google can be powerful tools to identify volunteer groups, charities, and non-profits that align with your interests.

Beyond basic searches, there are dedicated platforms designed to connect individuals with service opportunities both locally and globally. Websites such as VolunteerMatch, Idealist, and Doit.life offer comprehensive databases of volunteer roles, making it easier to find opportunities that fit your skills, availability, and passion. These platforms can also introduce you to fresh opportunities and untapped channels you may not have previously considered.

Combining traditional networking with online research ensures you are exposed to a wide range of service opportunities, increasing your chances of finding the right fit.

Finding a Mentor

While online research and networking can help you discover service opportunities, having a mentor can provide invaluable guidance and encouragement as you navigate your journey. Finding an inspirational person in your community with experience in your area of interest is an excellent first step. A mentor can offer advice, share lessons from their own path, and help you refine your approach to service.

Seek out mentorship opportunities by building genuine connections with those who have significantly impacted the field you're interested in. Attending networking events, conferences, or workshops can also help you engage with potential mentors who can provide insight and support.

In my early political career, which began in 2006, I had the invaluable support of Councillor Margaret Jones, my mentor at the time. She had a remarkable history of public service, having served as Thurrock Borough Council's first mayor in 1974 and dedicating 45 years to her role as a councillor before retiring in 2008. Her guidance shaped my approach to public service, teaching me the importance of resilience, integrity, and dedication to the community.

Having a mentor can be transformative, but just as important is the opportunity to pay it forward by mentoring others. As I progressed in my political career, I made it a priority to support aspiring leaders. One memorable experience was mentoring a young woman who approached me at just 17 years old, eager to learn about politics. I took her along with me to meet the electorate, teaching her how to campaign effectively and engage with her community. At 19, Councillor Cici Mamwa was elected as a young councillor in Thurrock. Seeing her take on that role was a proud moment, proof that mentorship can shape the next generation of leaders.

Having a mentor is particularly valuable when stepping into unfamiliar territory or taking on a volunteer position for the first time. Learning from those who have gone before you can accelerate your growth, provide essential guidance, and build your confidence. Many institutions recognise this and have formal mentoring initiatives. For example, newly appointed magistrates in their first year of service are paired with mentors who help them develop the necessary skills and competences for dispensing justice. This structured support system ensures they receive the guidance needed to settle into their judicial office effectively.

While having a dedicated mentor in your specific field is valuable, you can learn from role models by observing them from afar. Follow their social media profiles, engage with their content, and study their approach to leadership. Even without direct mentorship, you can gain inspiration and practical knowledge from the experience they share.

Investing in Personal Development

Mentorship and networking provide valuable guidance, but ultimately, preparing for service roles requires a commitment to personal growth. Focusing on self-improvement is one of the best ways to equip yourself for opportunities to serve others effectively. Continuous learning broadens your horizons, builds new skills, and strengthens your ability to make an impact.

There are many ways to invest in personal development, both formally and informally. Attending seminars, webinars, and workshops can deepen your knowledge in a particular field, while online learning platforms like Udemy offer a wide range of courses to help you develop expertise at your own pace. If you're interested in acquiring professional qualifications, pursuing certifications in leadership, governance, or community development can enhance your ability to contribute meaningfully.

Building Your Profile

Investment in personal development equips you with the knowledge and skills needed to serve effectively, but to maximise your impact, you must be intentional about building your profile. Whether you aspire to be a politician or community leader, establishing a strong public presence helps you connect with supporters and position yourself as a credible voice.

Start by clearly communicating your values and interests to your target audience. Consider developing an online presence through platforms like LinkedIn, where you can share your insights, engage with thought leaders, and showcase your commitment to service. Writing blog posts, contributing to discussions, and using social media can further amplify your message.

To strengthen your profile, you might also consider creating a personal website or enlisting a professional to help you craft a polished online presence. Social media platforms such as Instagram, Facebook, and Twitter can be powerful tools for growing your personal brand and engaging with a wider audience. Strategic self-promotion isn't about vanity; it's about ensuring that your message reaches the people who need to hear it.

Summary of Chapter 2: Preparing for a Life of Service

- **Discovering Your Purpose**: Identifying your core motivations and passions helps align your service efforts with your values, ensuring a more meaningful and impactful contribution to society.
- **Setting Clear Goals**: Establishing specific objectives helps direct your actions, prioritize opportunities, and focus your energy on achieving tangible results in your chosen service roles.
- **Building a Network**: Networking with like-minded individuals and mentors provides valuable support, guidance, and opportunities to amplify your impact while learning from others' experiences.
- **Seeking Mentorship**: A mentor offers crucial advice, encouragement, and practical knowledge to navigate your service journey and can inspire you to pay it forward by mentoring others.
- **Investing in Personal Development**: Continuously improving your skills and expanding your knowledge helps you grow as a leader while building your personal profile enhances your ability to influence and engage others in your mission.

Chapter 3

Core Skills for Impactful Service

I have seen a volunteer from community organisation step in to help a struggling family. He wasn't doing it for recognition or personal gain. He simply saw a need and acted. He listened with empathy, connected the family with resources, and rallied others to offer support. It wasn't his title that made the difference; it was the ability to communicate, adapt, and lead with compassion.

Not every act of service requires formal expertise or special skills. Sometimes, a kind word, a helping hand, or simply showing up is enough to create an impact.

But as you step into roles that require greater responsibility, whether as a Member of Parliament (MP), a councillor, a religious leader, a school governor shaping young minds, a magistrate ensuring justice, or a non-executive director guiding organisations, certain skills become essential.

In this section, we'll explore the core abilities that elevate service from good intention to meaningful change: the power of communication, the warmth of empathy, the strength of adaptability, and the brilliance of leadership. These qualities turn ordinary people into extraordinary leaders in positions of influence, driving meaningful change.

Whether you're stepping into a leadership role or simply looking to contribute more effectively to your community, developing these skills will set you apart and enhance the impact of your service.

Communication Skills

Effective communication is critical for acts of service roles because it allows leaders to clearly communicate their vision, goals, and policies to various stakeholders. Being a good communicator allows politicians, councillors, and public servants to connect with their constituents, understand their needs, and address their concerns. This ability is equally useful for religious leaders, school governors, and community activists who want to collaborate and promote community unity.

Empathy and Compassion

While performing acts of service, one frequently interacts with individuals coping with various difficulties. Leaders need to possess the qualities of empathy and compassion to genuinely comprehend the requirements and challenges others face. Empathetic leaders can develop trust and promote an environment that is supportive and welcoming in their respective areas of influence.

Problem-Solving Skills

Leaders who perform acts of service are frequently confronted with complex issues and challenges that necessitate effective problem-solving abilities. The ability to analyse situations, think critically, and develop creative solutions is essential for overcoming obstacles and achieving positive results.

Negotiation and Conflict Resolution

Negotiation and conflict resolution are essential skills for roles in politics, community leadership, and non-executive directors. To successfully navigate competing interests, mediate disputes, and find common ground among relevant parties with opposing viewpoints, leaders must develop these abilities.

A skilled negotiator can drive progress and positive change by promoting consensus and facilitating cooperation.

Decision-Making Abilities

The decisions made by leaders can have wide-ranging effects, shaping communities, organisations, and individual lives. Those in these leadership roles must develop strong decision-making skills to deal with complex challenges with confidence and integrity. Effective leaders carefully assess multiple factors, consider the potential impact on those they serve, and make choices that are both well-informed and aligned with their core values and long-term goals. Thoughtful, strategic decision-making is not just a skill but a responsibility ensuring positive and lasting change.

Strategic Thinking

Taking on service roles frequently necessitates engaging in long-term planning and strategic thinking. Leaders need to be able to see what lies ahead and devise plans that will allow them to accomplish their objectives most efficiently. The ability to anticipate challenges, recognise opportunities, and adapt to changing circumstances is essential to strategic thinking.

Interpersonal Skills

For leaders to be successful in building strong relationships with constituents, colleagues, and the wider community, strong interpersonal skills are necessary. These abilities include active listening, collaboration, networking, and rapport building, all of which contribute to efficient teamwork and accomplishing shared goals. Leaders who master these abilities create environments where ideas thrive, partnerships flourish, and collective success becomes possible.

Integrity and Ethical Conduct

When it comes to leadership roles in public service, having integrity is a quality that cannot be compromised. Upholding high ethical standards builds trust and establishes credibility and reliability within the community.

Leaders who demonstrate unwavering integrity set a powerful example, inspiring others to act with honesty, fairness, and accountability. By leading with strong moral principles, they cultivate a culture of trust and ethical behaviour that strengthens both their influence and the communities they serve.

Resilience and Perseverance

Criticism, mistakes, and difficulties are common experiences for those in leadership roles serving the public. Even in the face of challenges, it is possible to keep one's concentration and sense of purpose alive with the help of traits such as resilience and perseverance. These characteristics allow leaders to overcome setbacks and keep moving forward in pursuing their objectives.

Emotional Intelligence

Self-awareness, self-control, empathy, and the ability to interact effectively with others are all components of emotional intelligence. Leaders with high emotional intelligence can understand and effectively manage their own emotions, enabling them to handle stressful situations better and connect with others on a deeper level.

Adaptability and Flexibility

Participation in acts of service typically occurs in dynamic and constantly evolving environments. Leaders must be adaptable and versatile in their approach, welcoming change and maintaining an open mind to ideas. Because of this, they can respond proactively to new problems and seize opportunities for personal development and advancement.

Public Speaking and Presentation Skills

Leaders in public life, politics, and governance must often step into the spotlight and address audiences of all sizes. Communicating effectively through public speaking or presentation is crucial for inspiring, persuading, and engaging others. A strong, confident delivery can capture attention, convey powerful messages, and motivate people to take action. This means encouraging them to listen and feeling compelled to respond, whether by supporting a cause, changing their behaviour, or getting involved in a project. By using the right words, tone, and body language, leaders can encourage enthusiasm and guide their audience towards meaningful steps that lead to tangible outcomes.

Financial Literacy and Budget Management

Financial literacy and the ability to manage a budget are required skills for many leadership roles, including non-executive directors and school governors. The ability to understand financial reports, develop and manage budgets, and make informed financial decisions is directly linked to the successful allocation of resources and the completion of projects and initiatives. Financially savvy leaders ensure that their organisations stay on track, maximise their impact, and achieve their goals with allocated resources. This skill is key to sustaining growth, ensuring accountability, and long-term success.

Inclusivity and Diversity Awareness

To fulfil their roles as leaders, public officeholders must engage with diverse groups of people, each bringing their own unique experiences, cultures, and perspectives. By prioritising inclusivity and demonstrating a deep awareness of diversity, leaders create an environment where everyone feels valued and respected. This approach promotes a sense of belonging among their followers, ensuring that all voices are heard and considered. Leaders who champion inclusivity strengthen their communities and inspire greater collaboration, innovation, and collective progress.

Leadership

Becoming an influential leader is a journey that can touch every part of our lives because leadership is not just about holding a position or title; it's about how we interact with others, make decisions, and inspire change.

Leadership is a key theme throughout this book, and you'll notice its repetition because it's essential to every act of service. Whether in politics or other public life roles, leadership involves guiding others towards a shared vision, gaining support, and inspiring desired change.

Effective leaders possess a range of qualities, such as charisma, emotional intelligence, and a clear vision for the future. They also can make tough decisions, often in high-pressure situations.

Impactful Leaders: The WISE Approach

As we've seen, leadership shapes how we connect with others, make decisions, and drive change. But what truly makes a leader impactful? I like to call it WISE leadership. It is a concept that redefines leadership beyond just a title or role. It's a journey guided by four core values: **Wisdom, Integrity, Systems Thinking, and Empathy**. These principles not only shape how leaders serve but also empower them to create lasting, positive change within communities and beyond.

Whether you are a community champion, councillor, MP, or someone in the public eye, embodying WISE leadership can elevate your acts of service and amplify your impact.

Each element of WISE Leadership contributes to building a foundation for impactful leadership. Let's explore the core qualities that shape a WISE leader and how they can elevate your service.

1. Wisdom: Your Guiding Compass

Wisdom in leadership is about making sound, thoughtful decisions that serve the greater good. It's not about knowing everything but knowing enough to ask the right questions and to consider perspectives beyond your own. Think of wisdom as a compass guiding you through the complexities of leadership. A wise leader understands when to act, when to listen, and when to seek counsel. By embracing continuous learning and reflection, you become equipped to make choices that have a positive and lasting impact.

2. Integrity: Building Trust and Credibility

Integrity is the cornerstone of WISE leadership. Without it, trust and respect are lost, and the potential to inspire others diminishes. A leader with integrity is transparent, honest, and consistent in their actions and values. Integrity doesn't mean perfection; it means taking responsibility for mistakes, communicating openly, and staying true to your values. When leaders consistently demonstrate integrity, they earn the trust and loyalty of those they serve.

3. Systems Thinking: Connecting the Dots

Effective leaders see societies and communities as interconnected systems, each action and decision influencing a broader web of people and outcomes. Systems thinking helps leaders understand how policies, community initiatives, or any changes affect the bigger picture. By considering the ripple effects of your actions, you can design and implement changes that have positive, far-reaching impacts. This holistic approach allows WISE leaders to create sustainable and inclusive solutions.

4. Empathy: Leading with Compassion

Empathy is the heart of WISE leadership. It's about placing yourself in others' shoes, understanding their needs, and connecting with their experiences. Empathetic leaders build strong, supportive relationships with those they serve, promoting an environment where everyone feels valued. By leading with empathy, you cultivate a culture of respect and compassion, which is essential for any leader seeking to make a positive impact.

Applying WISE Leadership in Your Service

Applying WISE leadership means integrating these values into your daily leadership practices.

Leading with wisdom means using sound judgement, drawing from both experience and knowledge to make informed, thoughtful decisions. To fully embrace this quality, take time to reflect on your actions and decisions regularly. Ask yourself, "What can I learn from this situation?" or "How will this decision affect others?" Consider the broader consequences of your choices and evaluate whether they align with your values and long-term goals. By continuously reflecting on your decisions, you ensure that your leadership remains grounded in wisdom, helping you deal with challenges with understanding and clarity.

Acting with integrity means upholding honesty, transparency, and ethical principles, which builds trust and credibility in relationships and actions. Strive to align your words and actions, ensuring consistency in everything you do. Be open about the reasons behind your decisions, and when mistakes occur, acknowledge them openly. This transparency strengthens trust and reinforces credibility. Ask yourself, "Am I communicating honestly, even when it's difficult?" "Am I taking responsibility for my mistakes and learning from them? "Are my actions consistently aligned with my stated values and principles?" By embracing these practices, you lead with integrity, building strong and trustworthy connections.

Thinking systematically means taking a holistic view of situations, understanding the interconnections and dependencies between different areas, and seeking solutions that benefit the larger system, recognising that actions in one area often have ripple effects on others. For example, a decision to improve local public transportation can influence employment opportunities, access to education, and overall community well-being. Ask yourself, "Who and what will be affected by this change?" "What are the potential ripple effects of my decision, and how might it impact the wider community?" "How can I encourage a collaborative approach that considers various perspectives?" By thinking systematically, you ensure your decisions contribute to broader, sustainable solutions.

Empathetic engagement means showing understanding and compassion for others' perspectives, creating a supportive environment that values individual experiences and encourages connection. Make time to listen actively to those you serve. Practice viewing situations from their point of view, which strengthens relationships and helps you address real needs. Ask yourself, "How can I actively listen to understand others' perspectives?" "Am I demonstrating patience and respect in difficult conversations?" "How often am I engaging with my community to stay connected to their needs and experiences?" By engaging empathetically, you build deeper connections for meaningful impact.

Overcoming Challenges with WISE Leadership

Leading with WISE principles doesn't mean there won't be challenges, but it does provide tools for overcoming them.

Navigating Complex Decisions:

Sometimes, decisions will require choosing between two equally valid options. In these moments, wisdom is crucial in helping you evaluate which option aligns best with long-term goals and community values. It's about considering the broader impact of each option, ensuring that the decision you make is thoughtful and supports the greater good.

Upholding Integrity Under Pressure:

There will be times when doing the right thing isn't easy or popular. Staying grounded in integrity is essential during these moments, as it helps you remain consistent, even when facing criticism or opposition. Upholding your ethical principles, even when difficult, builds trust and strengthens your leadership by showing that your values are unwavering.

Addressing Interconnected Issues

Systems thinking enables you to handle challenges that affect multiple sectors. For example, addressing youth unemployment requires a holistic approach, considering job opportunities, education, economic policies, and family support systems. By recognising the interconnections between different areas, you can create more comprehensive solutions with a far-reaching, positive impact.

Building Resilience Through Empathy

Leadership can be draining, especially when you're guiding others through crises or difficult times. Empathy is a key factor in building resilience, as it helps you stay focused on the greater purpose of serving others with compassion. By understanding and sharing in the struggles of those you lead, you develop the emotional strength to persevere, supporting those around you.

The Long-Term Impact of WISE Leadership

The impact of WISE leadership reaches well beyond individual projects or initiatives. Leaders guided by Wisdom, Integrity, Systems Thinking, and Empathy create a lasting legacy; they don't just serve; they inspire others to serve as well, leaving a positive and enduring mark on the world.

Creating a Culture of Trust and Accountability:

When leaders act with integrity, they inspire confidence in the system they represent. People are more likely to engage positively within the community when they trust that their leaders are honest, transparent, and committed to doing the right thing. By leading with integrity, leaders set the tone for a culture of accountability, where everyone is held to the same high standards, resulting in stronger, more collaborative communities.

Inspiring the Next Generation:

WISE leaders serve as role models for the next generation, demonstrating the power of empathy, compassion, and thoughtful decision-making. By embodying these values in their actions, they show that service to others is impactful and deeply rewarding. This example inspires young leaders to follow in their footsteps, perpetuating a legacy of positive change and leadership that prioritises the well-being of others.

Building Resilient, Interconnected Communities:

WISE leaders understand that communities are interconnected in complex ways. They recognise that decisions made in one area can have ripple effects throughout the community. With this understanding, they make choices that strengthen community ties, building resilience and unity. By nurturing connections and addressing the needs of all parts of the community, they help build a society that can weather challenges and thrive together.

Leaving a Lasting Impact:

Leaders who practice WISE leadership leave more than just policies or infrastructure behind; they leave a lasting culture of empathy, trust, and holistic thinking. These leaders create environments where future generations can build on the values of service, collaboration, and integrity. The impact of their leadership endures through the people they inspire and the positive changes they make in the communities they serve.

Summary of Chapter 3: Core Skills for Impactful Service

- **Essential Leadership Skills**: Successful service requires core skills like effective communication, empathy, adaptability, and leadership, which turn good intentions into meaningful change in various roles, such as councillors, MPs, and religious leaders.
- **Communication and Empathy**: Strong communication and empathy are crucial for leaders to connect with individuals, address concerns, and build trust while also creating a supportive and inclusive environment for diverse communities.
- **Problem-Solving and Conflict Resolution**: Leaders must develop problem-solving abilities, negotiation skills, and conflict-resolution strategies to navigate complex challenges, mediate disputes, and make informed decisions that benefit the broader community.
- **Strategic and Ethical Decision-Making**: Effective leaders employ strategic thinking and decision-making skills to assess long-term impacts, ensuring their choices align with core values and community needs while maintaining integrity and ethical conduct.
- **The WISE Leadership Approach**: WISE leadership (Wisdom, Integrity, Systems Thinking, and Empathy) redefines leadership by emphasising holistic, compassionate decision-making and a commitment to long-term, sustainable community impact.

Chapter 4
Leading with Confidence

The first time I spoke at a planning committee as a councillor representing residents, I knew the responsibility I carried. I had prepared extensively, researching the case, reviewing residents' concerns, and structuring my arguments clearly. As I stood up and prepared to speak, I felt a deep sense of purpose. This was my chance to ensure that the voices of my community were heard where it mattered most.

I confidently presented the case, articulating the impact the proposed development would have on local residents. I spoke with clarity and conviction, ensuring that every point was backed by evidence and the genuine concerns of the people I represented. As I delivered my argument, I saw the committee members listening intently and engaging with the points I raised. By the time I finished, it was clear that the message had resonated, and meaningful discussions followed.

Strong communication, time management, and the ability to influence others are essential to delivering impactful service in public office. Whether addressing a committee, engaging with the media, or contributing to important conversations, these skills determine your effectiveness as a leader. Equally important is the capacity to listen and empathise, understanding the needs of the people you represent to drive real change.

Public service is a continuous learning experience. Every challenge, debate, and decision allows you to refine your skills and approach. By embracing growth, enhancing your time management, public speaking, and media engagement, you strengthen your influence and impact. The more you invest in these abilities, the more effectively you can champion causes, inspire, and lead.

Communicating More Effectively

Whether you are a councillor, a member of parliament, or in any role involving public or stakeholder engagement, strong communication is essential for delivering real impact. The ability to actively listen, use clear and accessible language, adapt messages to the audience, and engage in open, two-way dialogue builds trust and strengthens connections. Every interaction is a chance to inspire change and make a lasting difference.

Listening is as important as speaking. Paying attention to the concerns of community members, volunteers, or colleagues shows respect and helps you understand their needs. A councillor who listens carefully during a public meeting, for example, is better equipped to push for policies that reflect local priorities. Clarity in messaging is equally crucial. Using straightforward language instead of jargon ensures your message resonates, whether in council chambers, media interviews, or community discussions. Explaining policy change in a way that connects to people's daily lives makes information more accessible and relevant.

Trust is built through transparency. Being honest about challenges, limitations, and potential outcomes strengthens credibility, whether addressing budget constraints, policy changes, or community concerns. If a local project faces funding difficulties, acknowledging the issue and working together on solutions encourages constructive dialogue. Empathy further strengthens relationships, allowing leaders to connect on a human level. Addressing public safety concerns while outlining concrete steps reassures residents that their voices matter.

Using multiple communication channels enhances engagement. Social media enables quick updates and interaction, while newsletters, public meetings, and community events allow for deeper discussion. Each method serves a different audience, ensuring a broader reach. Non-verbal communication also plays a key role. Body language, tone, and facial expressions can reinforce or weaken a message. Maintaining an open and approachable demeanour, particularly in face-to-face interactions, builds rapport and trust. A simple smile or engaged posture can significantly affect how a message is received.

Consistency reinforces your goals and vision. Repeating core messages across different platforms ensures they are understood and remembered. If environmental protection is a priority, integrating this commitment into speeches, articles, and discussions underscores your dedication. In diverse communities, cultural awareness is also essential. Respecting different norms and practices when engaging with constituents or colleagues promotes inclusivity and strengthens relationships.

Finally, effective communication requires follow-through. Delivering on commitments, responding to concerns, and keeping people informed builds lasting trust. Whether leading a community initiative or shaping policy, being reliable in your communications enhances your ability to lead with confidence and influence.

Mastering Time Management in a Busy Role

Time management is essential for balancing responsibilities and making a meaningful impact, whether you are a councillor, a member of parliament, a community volunteer, a church worker, a public appointee, or a non-executive director. Managing multiple commitments effectively requires a strategic approach to prioritising, planning, and maintaining focus.

Not all tasks hold the same level of urgency or importance, so it's crucial to assess and organise them accordingly. Using frameworks like the Eisenhower Matrix helps distinguish between urgent and important tasks, allowing you to address pressing matters while scheduling or delegating others. For example, preparing for a board meeting may be important but not urgent until the deadline nears, at which point it becomes a top priority. By structuring your workload in this way, you can avoid last-minute stress and stay on top of key responsibilities.

Planning ahead is another fundamental aspect of effective time management. Whether through a digital calendar or a physical planner, specific time slots for meetings, reports, and community engagements ensure a more structured and productive schedule. An MP, for instance, might dedicate set hours each week to parliamentary duties, constituents' meetings, and media engagement, ensuring each responsibility receives adequate attention.

Technology can further enhance efficiency, offering tools that streamline scheduling, communication, and task management. Digital calendars help magistrates track court sittings, allocate time for case preparation, and manage judicial training, ensuring punctuality and preparedness. Embracing such tools allows for greater organisation and smoother workflow.

Setting clear goals is another way to stay on track. Defining objectives and breaking them into actionable steps ensures steady progress. If the aim is to improve the local environment, scheduling monthly clean-up events and allocating time for planning and execution makes the initiative more achievable. Regularly reflecting on priorities and adjusting strategies ensures that efforts remain aligned with long-term goals.

While taking on multiple roles can be fulfilling, overcommitting can lead to burnout and diminished effectiveness. Recognising personal limits and knowing when to decline additional responsibilities helps maintain balance. A church worker, for instance, may choose to focus on key commitments rather than volunteering at every event to ensure contributions remain impactful. Similarly, a non-executive director might turn down opportunities not aligning with their expertise or organisational objectives.

Punctuality is another crucial element of professional and community work. Arriving early to meetings or events demonstrates respect for others' time and helps prevent unnecessary delays. Simple strategies, such as scheduling a

6 p.m. meeting as 5.50 p.m. in your diary, create a buffer for unforeseen circumstances and ensure a timely start.

Ultimately, time management is an ongoing process that requires regular evaluation and adaptation. As responsibilities evolve, so should the strategies used to handle them. A councillor struggling to balance constituent work and council meetings might revise their schedule to dedicate more time to direct community engagement. By staying flexible and refining your approach, you can maintain efficiency, reduce stress, and enhance your ability to lead and serve effectively.

Growing Your Influence and Reach

Whether you're focused on personal growth, advancing your career, or leading an organisation for positive change, building and nurturing relationships is essential. A strong network can unlock resources, partnerships, and support, amplifying your impact on the causes you care about.

One of the most effective ways to grow your network is by joining professional organisations. Becoming a member gives you access to a structured platform for connecting with like-minded individuals and potential collaborators. For example, joining a medical association opens doors to valuable relationships, resources, and opportunities that can propel your goals in that field.

As mentioned previously, social media is a powerful tool for networking. Engaging on platforms like LinkedIn or joining online communities related to your interests allows you to connect with others virtually, often leading to real-world collaborations. If you are passionate about environmental conservation, for example, participating in eco-focused online groups can help you connect with organisations and individuals aligned with your mission.

In-person networking remains invaluable; however, attending conferences, workshops, and community events offers a unique opportunity to build face-to-face relationships. Whether it's attending community forums or participating in neighbourhood gatherings, these events provide a space to connect with local leaders and residents, helping you address shared goals.

The key to successful networking is authenticity. Focus on cultivating genuine connections, not just seeking immediate benefits. Engage with people sincerely and enthusiastically, whether at a charity event or a professional seminar. These authentic interactions promote trust and lead to long-lasting, valuable relationships.

Maintaining relationships requires ongoing efforts. After meeting someone, follow up with a thoughtful message or email expressing your appreciation and exploring future opportunities for collaboration. Sharing updates, resources, or ideas of mutual interest keeps the connection alive and shows your commitment.

Finally, offer mutual value by sharing your expertise, offering guidance, or introducing others to helpful resources. This strengthens your relationships and positions you as a valuable ally. For instance, volunteering your skills in event planning for a non-profit organisation can contribute meaningfully while establishing you as a trusted collaborator.

Speaking with Confidence: Public Speaking Tips

Public speaking is a powerful way to share your message, inspire action, and build support for community initiatives. Whether delivering a speech, leading a discussion, or rallying people behind a cause, effective communication is key. While some individuals have a natural flair for public speaking, others refine their skills through training and practice. Organisations like *Toastmasters* prove that great speakers are made, not just born.

Even experienced public figures recognise the importance of professional guidance. The late Margaret Thatcher, former UK Prime Minister, famously undertook private elocution lessons before her 1979 election to develop a more authoritative vocal presence and strengthen her confidence. Her example underscores how impactful communication can shape public perception and leadership success. As Anthony Robbins aptly put it: "People are rewarded in public for what they practice for years in private."

Confidence in speaking begins with understanding your audience. Tailoring your message to their interests, needs, and backgrounds ensures a stronger connection and lasting impact. For example, when speaking to young people about environmental protection, focusing on how their efforts directly contribute to a healthier planet makes the message more relatable and compelling. Structuring content effectively also plays a crucial role. A speech should open with a compelling introduction, present key points with engaging examples, and conclude with a memorable takeaway. If discussing volunteer work at an animal shelter, starting with a heartfelt story about a rescued animal, outlining ways to contribute, and ending with a powerful call to action can create a lasting impression.

Regular practice builds confidence and improves delivery. Rehearsing in front of a mirror, with friends, or by recording oneself helps refine pace, tone, and body language. Like preparing for a workshop or presentation, consistent practice transforms nervous energy into poise and clarity. Speaking at smaller gatherings, such as team meetings or local events, provides valuable experience before addressing larger audiences. Engaging the audience is equally important. Maintaining eye contact, using open body language, and incorporating interactive elements create a lively connection. Personal stories and thought-provoking questions make speeches more memorable while adjusting tone, pace, and gesture enhances impact.

Visual aids can further amplify a message when used wisely. Slides, images, or props should be clear and relevant, reinforcing key points rather than overwhelming the audience with excessive information. When promoting a charity event, for instance, showing compelling images of past initiatives and beneficiaries can strengthen emotional appeal. However, authenticity remains the most powerful tool in public speaking. Genuine passion, honesty, and personal experiences make messages resonate deeply. If supporting homeless outreach, sharing the story of what inspired the cause creates trust and engagement.

Managing nervousness is essential, as even the most seasoned speakers experience it. Channeling that energy into enthusiasm, taking deep breaths before stepping on stage, and visualising success all help cultivate confidence. Learning from accomplished speakers through platforms like TED Talks or YouTube offers valuable insights into delivery, stage presence, and audience engagement. Observing their techniques and adapting effective strategies to suit different contexts refine one's speaking style over time.

Ultimately, mastering public speaking is an ongoing journey of preparation, practice, and refinement. Each opportunity to speak is a chance to inspire, influence, and create a lasting impact.

Maximising Impact in Meetings

Maximising your impact in meetings requires more than just attendance. It demands preparation, active participation, and a commitment to the organisation's success. Meetings serve as essential platforms for decision-making and strategic planning, and how you contribute shapes both outcomes and your credibility within the organisation. Arriving on time sets the right tone, demonstrates respect for others, and ensures discussions remain productive. Being well-prepared by reviewing agendas, reports, and relevant documents equips you to offer meaningful insights. For example, familiarising yourself with financial reports before a discussion enables you to ask informed questions and propose effective solutions.

Understanding your role helps you align your contributions effectively, whether in governance, strategy, or finance. Actively participating in discussions, sharing unique perspectives, and asking thoughtful questions facilitates richer conversations and better decision-making. If you have legal or technological expertise, using that knowledge to highlight overlooked aspects strengthens the discussion. Engaging respectfully, listening attentively, and considering different viewpoints enhances collaboration and maintains professionalism, even in moments of disagreement.

Staying fully engaged is essential. Avoid distractions and keep your contributions clear and concise. Thoughtful questions can spark valuable discussions and lead to innovative ideas. Confidentiality must be maintained, particularly when handling sensitive information, thus preserving trust and integrity.

Following up on action items reinforces your reliability. Reviewing decisions, fulfilling commitments promptly, and keeping stakeholders informed demonstrate dedication and accountability. Continuous learning strengthens your ability to add fresh perspectives, so staying informed about trends and best practices will enable you to bring fresh perspectives to discussions. Your engagement, preparation, and follow-through ultimately determine the value you bring, solidifying your role as a trusted and effective person.

Mastering Media Interviews

Being interviewed by the media is like delivering a public speech. It's an opportunity to share your message, highlight your contributions, and inspire others. Whether you're involved in politics, community initiatives, volunteer work, or tackling social issues, a confident and engaging delivery can amplify your voice and make your cause resonate with a wider audience. Understanding the media outlet and its audience helps tailor your message effectively. Tailor your message to align with their interests and priorities. Speaking to a local news station, for instance, requires an emphasis on community impact, whereas addressing a broader audience calls for highlighting universal values that connect with diverse viewers.

Clarity is key. Craft a concise and impactful core message. This should encapsulate the heart of your cause in a few sentences. For instance, promoting a neighbourhood clean-up could be summarised as: *"We're coming together to create a cleaner, healthier environment for everyone in our community."*

Keeping responses concise ensures your points remain sharp and impactful. Avoiding jargon or overly complex language helps maintain accessibility, ensuring your message reaches and resonates with as many people as possible.

Nonverbal communication also plays a crucial role. Maintaining good posture and eye contact and eliminating distractions like fidgeting enhance credibility. Virtual interviews require additional preparation. Checking camera angles, lighting, and audio in advance ensures a professional presence.

Staying composed under pressure is essential, and pausing to gather thoughts can convey confidence rather than hesitation. Even when faced with difficult questions, honesty and composure strengthen your position. Acknowledging challenges while steering the conversation towards solutions and achievements keeps the narrative positive and forward-focused.

Interviewers may sometimes deviate from the topic, but gently redirecting the conversation to key points reinforces the message. Maintaining an enthusiastic and optimistic tone encourages engagement, and expressing gratitude at the end of an interview leaves a lasting positive impression. A simple thank-you to the interviewer and media outlet reinforces goodwill and strengthens relationships, paving the way for future opportunities to share and grow your cause.

Enhancing your Interpersonal Skills

Building strong interpersonal skills is essential for anyone involved in public service. These skills enable you to connect with others, appreciate diverse cultures, and respond effectively to their needs. Your ability to engage with people can significantly enhance your leadership performance. Understanding the individuals or groups you aim to serve is the first step in building trust. Taking the time to listen to their concerns, aspirations, and challenges ensures that your efforts are both relevant and impactful. Attending community meetings, conducting surveys, and holding open forums helps develop a clear understanding of community priorities. For instance, when working on a neighbourhood improvement project, speaking directly with residents can reveal pressing issues, such as the need for safer streets or better recreational spaces.

Interacting with diverse groups requires cultural awareness and a willingness to embrace different perspectives. Demonstrating respect for various customs, traditions, and beliefs creates an inclusive environment that strengthens relationships. Simple gestures, like learning about the significance of cultural practices or participating in community events, show a commitment to inclusivity. Communication is crucial in developing strong interpersonal connections, and adjusting your style to suit different audiences helps build rapport. Some individuals prefer direct and factual discussions, while others respond better to a more empathetic and personal approach. The ability to adjust ensures that messages are received clearly and effectively.

Empathy allows leaders to connect with people on a deeper level. Understanding and acknowledging different perspectives builds trust and encourages support for initiatives. Active listening, showing genuine concern, and remaining open to different experiences go a long way in strengthening relationships. Collaboration further increases impact, as working alongside other community leaders, organisations, and stakeholders leads to creative solutions and shared success. For example, organising a park clean-up becomes a more effective initiative when local businesses, schools, and environmental groups are involved.

Trust is the foundation of any strong relationship, and honouring commitments is essential to maintaining credibility. Following through on promises, whether addressing concerns or delivering solutions, demonstrates dedication and reliability. If a councillor pledges to hold regular advice surgeries, keeping that commitment reinforces trust within the community. Conflict resolution is another vital skill in public life. Disagreements are inevitable but resolving them constructively while focusing on shared goals helps maintain unity. Finding common ground and promoting respectful discussions allows for solutions that satisfy all parties involved.

Acknowledging and appreciating others' contributions strengthens connections and encourages collaboration. Whether through a simple thank-you note, public recognition, or a thoughtful gesture, expressing gratitude enhances goodwill and motivates continued support. Recognising the efforts of community members and partners contributes to a positive and cooperative environment, reinforcing the bonds that drive meaningful change.

Summary of Chapter 4: Leading with Confidence

- **Preparation and Clarity in Communication**: Effective leaders thoroughly prepare for public speaking or committee meetings by researching, structuring their arguments, and presenting with clarity and conviction, ensuring their message resonates with the audience.
- **Strong Communication Skills**: Leading with confidence requires active listening, clear and accessible language, and the ability to engage in two-way dialogue. Transparency, empathy, and the use of multiple communication channels (including social media and in-person meetings) build trust and influence.
- **Time Management**: Prioritising tasks, setting clear goals, and using tools like digital calendars enhance time management. Effective leaders balance multiple commitments by assessing urgency, planning ahead, and adjusting strategies to avoid burnout.
- **Networking and Relationship Building**: Growing influence involves networking through professional organisations, social media, and in-person events. Authenticity and mutual value in these relationships are key to long-term success and impact.
- **Mastering Public Speaking and Media Interviews**: Confidence in public speaking comes from understanding the audience, practicing regularly, and using non-verbal communication to reinforce the message. Handling media interviews effectively requires clarity, composure under pressure, and staying focused on key points.

Chapter 5

Awards for Extraordinary Service

A few years ago, I read about Tony Hudgell's story on the BBC's website. It was one of those moments that stopped you in your tracks and reminded you of the incredible power of determination and the impact one person can have, no matter how young.

Tony Hudgell, a five-year-old boy, had already endured more hardship than most people face in a lifetime. As a baby, he suffered horrific abuse that resulted in both of his legs being amputated. Yet, despite everything he had been through, Tony refused to be defined by his past. Instead, he set out to make a difference.

Inspired by Captain Tom Moore's legendary fundraising walk, Tony decided to take on his own challenge. His goal? To walk 10 kilometres on his new prosthetic legs and raise £500 for Evelina London Children's Hospital, the very place that saved his life.

At first, his steps were slow, unsteady. Each movement required effort, strength, and willpower beyond his years. But with every step, support for his cause grew. His story spread across the United Kingdom (UK), capturing hearts and inspiring thousands. Donations flooded in, and before long, the £500 target was left far behind. By the time Tony completed his challenge, he had raised an astonishing £1.7 million.

In recognition of his incredible determination and selflessness, Tony was awarded the British Empire Medal (BEM) in the 2024 New Year Honours, making him the youngest-ever recipient of this prestigious award.

His story is a powerful reminder that acts of service, regardless of how big or small, deserve to be recognised. Tony didn't set out for praise or awards. He simply wanted to give back to those who had helped him. But his actions made a difference in countless lives and inspired an entire nation to believe in the power of kindness, resilience, and service.

For decades, individuals from all backgrounds have been honoured for their dedication, hard work, and service, reflecting the nation's deep appreciation for those who make a difference. Beyond recognition, these awards inspire others to contribute to their communities. This chapter explores the significance of the British Royal Honours system, highlighting a few of those celebrated for their service and the role these awards play in encouraging excellence and generosity across the UK.

The British Royal Honours system is a longstanding tradition, which exists to recognise and reward primarily two categories of individuals. First, there are selfless givers who give of their time, wealth, or skills to the benefit of others for no immediate financial gain, such as community and charity workers, and there are those who are at the top of their chosen fields, such as prominent surgeons, lawyers, actors, and entrepreneurs.

These awards recognise people who have gone "above and beyond for the community or country." They would have made achievements in public life, committing themselves to serving the people or helping the nation. It is a powerful way to celebrate and encourage the spirit of service and achievements made by a wide range of citizens in several fields, including healthcare, education, charity, and other areas.

What it Means to Get a British Royal Honour:

People performing tremendous work for their communities often do so out of passion rather than seeking accolades or recognition. Receiving an award, on the other hand, is like receiving a pat on the back and demonstrating that other people appreciate what these individuals do.

Firstly, great privilege and prestige are associated with being listed on the King's Honours List. The award creates a legacy for individuals, marking their contributions for generations to come, in other words, immortalising the impact of their acts of service on the nation. Undoubtedly, receiving awards raises the profile of individuals who have dedicated their lives to serving others.

Secondly, receiving official recognition encourages recipients to continue carrying out their good works, resulting in a long-lasting beneficial effect on communities and society at large. It can also motivate people to strive constantly for excellence in their service to others. This public recognition shows how important it is to maintain high standards in public and community service.

In addition to encouraging individuals to persist in their efforts, acknowledgement and awards for exceptional conduct also inspire others to perform selfless acts, thereby creating a mindset of community engagement. Awardees become role models for others, encouraging positive social change and inspiring future generations. This means that other people can be inspired to emulate the dedication and commitment demonstrated by honourees, fostering a culture of unceasing service and excellence.

A knighthood ceremony.

Ranks of the British Honours

The varying levels of recognition given to individuals in the UK are based on their geographical impact, which can range from being of local to national importance. Local heroes receive the Member of the Order of the British Empire (MBE) for community contributions. Those with a wider regional influence may attain Officer of the Order of the British Empire (OBE). Commander of the Order of the British Empire (CBE) recognises honourees with national impact, while damehoods or knighthoods celebrate exceptional achievements at the highest level.

A DAMEHOOD OR A KNIGHTHOOD:

This is a top honour. You're looking for a preeminent contribution at a national or even international level, something widely recognised as a leading achievement with significant impact and a sustained contribution by the individual. Dr Margaret Ebunoluwa Aderin, M.B.E., the space scientist and Chancellor of the University of Leicester, received a damehood for her service to Science Education and Diversity in the 2024 New Year Honours list.

Commander of the Order of the British Empire (CBE):

This honour is awarded for a significant leading role at the regional level or for a contribution at the national level of a lesser degree. You can also get one for a distinguished, innovative contribution to any area of the UK. Rosamund Addo-Kissi-Debrah, Co-Founder and Chair of the Ella Roberta Family Foundation, received a CBE in 2023 for services to public health.

Officer of the Order of the British Empire (OBE):

The OBE is typically awarded to people who have made significant contributions to their communities or notable, nationally recognised professionals who have had a deep impact over a sustained period. In King Charles' first New Year Honours List in 2023, Hackney Councillor Susan Fajana-Thomas made OBE for her services to local government and gender equality.

Member of the British Empire (MBE):

This is awarded for service to a community, whether in a voluntary or charitable capacity or professional one. It is for making some sustained contribution but at a more limited level. This will have had a long-term, significant impact and stand out as an example to others. Marcus Rashford, footballer and campaigner for free school meals, received an MBE in 2021. Received MBE in recognition of his campaign to support vulnerable children during the COVID-19 pandemic. A drive for social change.

The Most Excellent Order of the British Empire medal.

British Empire Medal (BEM):

BEM focuses on recognising individuals who serve the community at the local level, whether through a particular institution, a school, or a church or in a special subject area where someone has identified a gap and filled it. Enyojo Opaluwa-Pinheiro, founder and chair of the Passenger Services BAME Network at the Department of Transport, received a BEM in 2023 for services to diversity and inclusion. The BEM can also be awarded to individuals who have made a significant local contribution but have not been doing so for long: for instance, young people in their teens and twenties, who had relatively limited service compared to some older persons who had been able to provide service over a longer length of time.

The King's Award for Voluntary Service (KAVS):

The KAVS is for outstanding achievement by groups that volunteer their own time to enhance and improve the quality of lives and opportunities of others in the local communities. It is the highest award given to volunteer groups across the UK. One of the organisations based in Thurrock, led by Yewande Kannike, The One Community Development Trust was established in 2008, and ten years later, in 2018, was honoured with this prestigious award, then known as the Queen's Award for Voluntary Service.

Nomination and Selection Process:

The Honours System offers two routes for nominations: public nominations and stakeholder suggestions. Public nominations are open to all members of the public, where anyone can propose a nomination for recognition. However, self-nominations are not allowed. On the other hand, the stakeholder suggestion method involves government departments designating an individual who oversees honours within their sectors. This designated person engages with key stakeholder bodies, such as charities, local government, and universities, to seek nominations for noteworthy individuals who have made exceptional contributions and deserve recognition for an honour. This collaborative approach to the nomination process ensures that deserving individuals are recognised for their hard work and contributions to society.

Independent Honours Committees:

After assessing the received nominations to check the legitimacy and correctness of the information provided in the nominations, as well as validating the nominees' details, the best nominations are forwarded to the relevant independent honours committees, which are separated by sector. These committees are based on different sectors of UK life: arts and media, community and voluntary service, the economy, education, health, parliamentary and political service, public service, science and technology, sports, and the state (civil service). Twice a year, they receive a big booklet containing hundreds of nominations for honours, which they assess and vote on based on factors such as the nominee's impact, dedication, and long-term commitment. The committee's recommendations are then forwarded to the Prime Minister and the King for approval before the Honours Secretariat writes to individuals to offer them an honour.

Writing a Nomination:

Individuals who perform acts of service cannot nominate themselves for personal recognition. Nominating individuals for awards is a positive way to recognise their contributions to improving people's lives, communities, and the nation. When writing a nomination, provide current information about the person's activities, their past accomplishments, and why they are significant. Include the geographical impact of your nominees' work in the nomination statement.

How Your Nominee Made a Difference:

You would need to explain what your nominee did to assist someone or fill a need. What would have happened if they hadn't been there? Even if other people perform similar roles, you should emphasise what distinguishes your person from others in the same roles. There may be expectations for their specific function, but what do they accomplish that goes beyond that? Why did they do that? Why was there a need, and who benefited? The people who make award decisions want to know about your nominee's narrative.

Factual Details Regarding the Nominee:

You will need to provide basic information about the nominees, such as their name, address, and date of birth (if you know it). Using this information, the Honours System will be able to verify your nominations and ensure that they are conducting the necessary checks.

Confidentiality:

The Data Protection Act provides an exemption for the honours procedure, allowing the system to collect information to consider someone for an honour. The individual submitting the nomination can supply information without the nominee knowing it. It is extremely advised that the individual being nominated be unaware of the nomination. If you speak with anyone who may be able to assist you with the nomination, keep it confidential so that the nominee is not aware. There is also a sense of surprise in the recognition, emphasising the genuineness of the acknowledgement. Being unaware will also keep nominees from feeling slighted if their nomination is unsuccessful due to the awards' competitive nature.

Geographical Impact:

One of the most important factors in determining whether someone deserves an honour is how their work affects others in their community. The level of the honour, from Damehood or Knighthood to MBE or BEM, is based on the geographical reach of their contributions. Include this information so that the committee can evaluate the individual's influence, assisting them in determining the appropriate level of honour.

Letters of Support (Public Nomination):

Two letters of support from individuals who know the nominee are to be included in the public nomination. Those familiar with the nominee's work and accomplishments and are willing and able to provide a letter of support will assist the Honours committee in better understanding the impact of the nominee's acts of service.

Useful links

The Cabinet Office:
www.gov.uk/honours
The Cabinet Office is in charge of managing the United Kingdom's honours system. Their website contains information on the various types of honours and awards available, including the Order of the British Empire (OBE), Knighthoods, and other prestigious honours.

The Honours and Appointments Secretariat:
https://honours.cabinetoffice.gov.uk

The Honours and Appointments Secretariat, part of the Cabinet Office, is responsible for the administration and processing of United Kingdom honours and awards. They provide information on the nomination and selection process, eligibility criteria, and various types of honours.

The London Gazette:
www.thegazette.co.uk
The London Gazette is the official public record for all state honours and awards. It publishes announcements about honours and awards, such as the New Year Honours and the King's Birthday Honours. The Gazette website allows you to search and view past honours and awards.

The Central Chancery of the Orders of Knighthood:
https://www.centralchancery.org.uk
The Central Chancery is responsible for the administration and issuing of honours and awards in the United Kingdom. It oversees the Order of the British Empire and other orders of chivalry.

Awards Intelligence:
www.awardsintelligence.co.uk

Awards Intelligence is an agency that provides professional support and advice to individuals and organisations seeking honours and awards. They offer services such as nominations, application writing, and strategic guidance throughout the honours process.

Summary of Chapter 5: Awards for Extraordinary Service

- **Tony Hudgell's Inspirational Story**: Tony, a five-year-old boy who overcame severe abuse and the loss of both legs, raised £1.7 million by walking 10 km on prosthetic legs to support Evelina London Children's Hospital. His story highlights the power of determination and service.
- **The British Royal Honours System**: The system recognises individuals who have made significant contributions to society, whether through selfless community work or outstanding achievements in various fields like healthcare, education, or public service.
- **Types of Awards and Recognition**: Awards range from the British Empire Medal (BEM) for local contributions to knighthoods and damehoods for national or international impact. Each level of recognition corresponds to the geographical reach and impact of an individual's service.
- **The Impact of Receiving an Honour**: Awards not only celebrate individual contributions but inspire continued service and encourage others to engage in acts of kindness and community involvement, fostering a culture of excellence and giving.
- **The Nomination and Selection Process**: Nominations for honours can be submitted publicly or through stakeholder suggestions. A thorough process involves assessment by independent committees, ensuring that deserving individuals are recognised for their lifelong dedication to service.

PART TWO

STARTING CLOSE TO HOME

Chapter 6

Home and Neighbours

One day, I met an elderly man who asked me where I was from and then struck up a conversation with me. Upon learning that I was from Nigeria, he began to share his own story. He said he had lived in the same area, one of the Essex neighbourhoods, for almost thirty years and that he had been alone since the death of his wife six years before. He spoke fondly of the Nigerians who had moved in next door a few years ago, describing them as friendly and helpful, something for which he was grateful. They kept an eye on him, did his shopping, and even put him on their Christmas gift list. In a way, they made him feel like he was part of their big family.

Being kind and helpful to others is an innate part of being human. We all have the desire to lend a helping hand, show interest, and make people feel better when they need it. While some people find it easy to assist others, some may be unsure how or where to begin.

Most of the time, acts of service are actions we perform for others without expecting anything in return. They can be as simple as holding a door open out of courtesy or as involved as volunteering at a local homeless shelter. These activities have the potential to significantly improve the lives of people and the communities in which they belong.

Serving your Family: Charity Begins at Home

The old saying "charity begins at home" is a timeless piece of advice that shows how important it is to encourage acts of service within the family. While the phrase usually refers to kindness and generosity, it can also be used to describe small acts of service that people do every day. Indeed, the home is the best place to learn to be kind and helpful.

The notion that charity starts at home is based on the idea that the values and behaviour taught within the family unit are the foundation for helping others in a broader sense. Serving your family teaches responsibility and empathy and allows individuals to understand how their actions affect those closest to them. Through acts of service at home, individuals develop essential skills such as cooperation, selflessness, and attentiveness.

In addition, the family unit represents the community, and the values of kindness and service taught within it spread to other places. Just as a pebble dropped into a pond makes waves get bigger and bigger, acts of compassion practised within the family can extend to neighbours, friends, and the broader society. This idea highlights the deep connection between personal and collective well-being.

Beyond the interpersonal benefits, promoting acts of service at home helps to create a more compassionate and selfless community. Children who watch and participate in acts of service within their families are more likely to maintain these beliefs into adulthood, resulting in a positive cycle of compassion and community involvement.

Parents serve their families by creating a safe and nurturing atmosphere where their children can grow to be loving, trustworthy, and healthy. Because each family is unique, the following examples of how to serve should be tailored to your family's specific needs and preferences.

Emotional Support:

Actively listening, validating feelings, and offering empathy create a foundation of trust within the family. A safe space for open communication allows everyone to share their thoughts and emotions without fear of judgement.

Quality Time:

Spending meaningful time together strengthens family bonds. Planning activities that everyone enjoys, whether it's a weekly game night or a monthly outing, helps create cherished traditions and lasting memories.

Education and Guidance:

Supporting children through challenges and helping them make informed decisions is a vital role of family members. Providing educational resources, assisting with homework, and encouraging curiosity contribute to their personal growth.

Financial Security:

Responsible and transparent financial management ensures stability for the family. Planning for the future through savings, investments, and education funds helps secure long-term well-being.

Home Management:

A well-maintained home creates a sense of order and comfort. Sharing household responsibilities and involving family members in age-appropriate chores lightens the load and instills responsibility and teamwork.

Health and Well-being:

Prioritising a healthy lifestyle benefits the entire family. Encouraging nutritious eating habits, regular exercise, and scheduling health check-ups ensure both physical and mental well-being. Addressing medical concerns promptly reinforces a proactive approach to health.

Problem Solving:

Teaching effective problem-solving skills equips children with the ability to approach life's challenges. Encouraging a mindset of resilience and teamwork enables family members to work together to find solutions.

Celebrating Achievements:

Acknowledging and celebrating accomplishments, no matter how big or small, promotes an environment of encouragement and motivation. Recognising each family member's successes reinforces a culture of appreciation and support.

Crisis Management:

Handling crises calmly and effectively helps keep the family stable. Offering comfort and taking care of each other's emotional and physical needs makes it easier to get through tough times together.

Personal Development:

Supporting both children and adults in learning and self-improvement helps the whole family grow. Encouraging new skills, hobbies, and personal goals creates a positive environment where everyone can develop and succeed together.

Cultural and Spiritual Guidance:

Passing down cultural and spiritual values instils a sense of identity and belonging. Engaging in traditions and activities that reinforce these values strengthens the family's connection to its heritage and beliefs.

Social Connections:

Building and maintaining positive relationships with extended family and friends creates a strong sense of community. Organising gatherings and social events helps strengthen family bonds and establish a supportive network beyond the household.

Acts of Love Towards Your Neighbours

Helping one's neighbours is like helping one's own family members. Luke 10:27 reminds us that to receive eternal life, we must love our neighbours as much as we love ourselves. This is a requirement for us to enter the kingdom of heaven. When you care about others, it is natural to want to do everything possible to help them. The biblical narrative of the Good Samaritan plainly states that the person you show love will regard you as a good neighbour. Being considered a good neighbour requires more than simply living next door to someone and keeping a reasonable distance from them.

Loneliness, social isolation, and economic hardship are some problems that come with modern life. Acts of service, which involve helping others in different ways, are an important part of human interaction. No matter how big or small, our involvement can make a difference in our neighbours' lives. By engaging with those around us, offering help, and supporting one another, we can strengthen our communities and create meaningful change. Here are some ideas for making a positive difference in your community and being a good neighbour:

Friendly Greetings:

A simple smile and greeting when you see your neighbours can make a big difference. Saying hello can brighten someone's day and help create a sense of community where people feel connected.

Regular Check-Ins:

It's important to check in on your neighbours, especially those who are elderly or live alone. A brief visit or even just a chat can help someone who might be feeling lonely or isolated, showing them that they're cared for.

Offering Practical Help:

Offering a helping hand with tasks like household chores, grocery shopping, or running errands can be incredibly valuable. Small actions like these can make a real difference in someone's life and lighten their load.

Community Events:

Taking part in or organising community events, like a neighbourhood picnic, book club, or gardening group, helps people connect and build a sense of belonging. These activities bring people together and strengthen community spirit.

Emergency Support:

It's important to be ready to support your neighbours during emergencies. Whether it's reaching out for outside help or offering direct assistance, being there in times of need shows solidarity and care.

Sharing Resources:

Generosity can go a long way, especially when sharing resources like food, clothing, or household items. Acts of kindness like these create a supportive environment and can ease financial burdens when times are tough.

Environmental Initiatives:

Joining environmental efforts like community clean-ups, tree planting, or neighbourhood improvement projects can make your area a better place. Working together on these initiatives helps the environment and builds stronger bonds between neighbours.

Crisis Support:

During difficult times, such as illness or loss, offering emotional support can make all the difference. A compassionate presence can provide comfort and strength, showing your neighbours they are not alone in their struggles.

Giving Back to Your Community

Communities come in various forms, ranging from our local neighbourhoods to global networks that connect us through shared interests and ideals. Each of us belongs to a different community, which could be defined by location, shared interests, cultural values, or common goals. Identifying with these diverse communities provides many opportunities to make a meaningful difference. It is both a privilege and a responsibility to give back to the communities that shape us.

Every community faces common issues that need to be addressed. Schools and colleges, for instance, are educational communities that value sharing information and experiences. Professional communities consist of people who collaborate and share common aims. Some individuals form groups based on shared interests or concerns, such as sports teams, book clubs, or environmental awareness groups. Small acts of service can have a big impact, creating a culture of kindness, unity, and positive change. What are some of the ways in which individuals can serve their communities?

Geographical Communities:

Geographical communities are neighbourhoods, towns, or cities where people live, work, and raise their children. Individuals who actively participate in acts of service help their communities. By devoting time and effort to the well-being of your community, you improve your quality of life and contribute to the general prosperity of your neighbourhood. You might be able to participate in local activities such as neighbourhood clean-ups, community gardens, and supporting local businesses. Volunteering at local shelters and organising community events are also effective methods to make a difference. Putting time and effort into the well-being of our surroundings helps to build a resilient, supportive, and healthy community.

Professional Communities:

Professional communities, which we build through our jobs, are also very important to our lives. Contributing to professional communities is a way to advance not only our own careers but also the success of the whole field. We can do this by working together on projects, mentoring other professionals, or participating in industry-related projects. In the workplace, acts of service can come in many forms, such as sharing knowledge, being a mentor, or actively participating in projects promoting diversity and inclusion.

Shared Interests and Passions:

Communities can be formed around common interests, causes, or hobbies, which is an excellent way to unite people. These communities are defined not by geography but by shared interests and passions, creating a sense of support and belonging. Members can help one another by sharing experiences, and those who contribute actively can make a positive difference while strengthening the group's unity. Acts of service, such as providing advice, planning events, or lending a helping hand, can strengthen these communities and enhance their impact.

Communities Based on Culture and Ethnicity:

Many individuals feel a strong connection to their ethnic and cultural origins, which are significant parts of their identity. They often come together as members of communities that celebrate shared traditions, values, and histories. Such communities offer a chance for people to learn from one another while promoting respect and understanding of different cultures. By embracing and preserving cultural diversity, individuals can build bridges and promote understanding among people from diverse backgrounds. They play an important role in creating harmony and appreciation for differences. Serving ethnic and cultural groups can take many forms, such as organising cultural events, participating in language preservation initiatives, or contributing to initiatives championing inclusion and diversity.

Global Communities:

In today's world, people are becoming more connected and involved in global communities that share common goals, such as preserving the environment, promoting human rights, or improving public health. Contributing to these communities can involve volunteering for international organisations, participating in advocacy campaigns, or supporting initiatives that tackle global challenges. By engaging in acts of service globally, individuals demonstrate their commitment to everyone's well-being.

Virtual Communities:

As technology advanced, online communities became more widespread and effective. These virtual spaces connect people worldwide, allowing them to communicate and interact via social media groups, forums, and even specific interest platforms. Individuals who participate in these online communities can make a positive impact, even if they are not present in person. People contribute by sharing relevant information, participating in debates, assisting others, or supporting charity initiatives.

Neighbourhood networks have developed alongside global internet communities, owing to platforms such as Facebook and the "Nextdoor" app. These platforms allow members to interact electronically and participate in their local communities. Volunteers in these local networks perform administrative responsibilities to keep things functioning smoothly. Participating in these networks is an excellent opportunity to devote your time to community service right in your own neighbourhood, ultimately contributing to the overall improvement of the area.

Summary of Chapter 6
Home and Neighbours

- **Acts of Kindness Strengthen Communities** – Small acts of service, such as assisting elderly neighbours, running errands, or offering companionship, can create a sense of belonging and support within local communities.
- **Charity Begins at Home** – The values of kindness, responsibility, and service are first cultivated within the family, shaping individuals' ability to contribute positively to society. By promoting compassion at home, these values naturally extend to neighbours and the wider community.
- **Being a Good Neighbour Matters** – Genuine neighbourly relationships involve more than just living side by side; they require active engagement, friendliness, and offering help when needed. Simple gestures like greetings, check-ins, and offering practical assistance can combat loneliness and isolation.
- **Serving Different Communities** – People belong to multiple communities: local, professional, cultural, and even global. Acts of service within each community, whether through mentorship, volunteering, or advocacy, contribute to collective well-being and positive change.
- **Leveraging Technology for Community Engagement** – Virtual and neighbourhood-based online communities provide opportunities for connection and service. Social media and local apps help individuals support one another, share resources, and build community spirit.

Chapter 7

Charitable Organisations

You may have heard of one of the following: Child Poverty Action Group, Centrepoint, Cancer Research UK, Oxfam, Save the Children, and the British Red Cross. These organisations play an important role in addressing challenges that improve the well-being of persons in need. They rely on donations, grants, and the passion of volunteers to keep their operations going.

Charities, also known as non-profit groups, contribute to the public welfare by addressing specific issues or causes rather than pursuing financial gain. In the United Kingdom, a wide range of voluntary and charity organisations work to address challenges such as poverty, homelessness, healthcare, and education.

Giving back to the community, whether through time, money, or other resources, is one of the most significant, satisfying, and rewarding things an individual can do. Volunteering with charitable organisations improves the world and enhances personal growth by providing a sense of purpose, fulfilment, and social connection. There are numerous compelling reasons why serving others through charitable organisations is important.

Charitable organisations work to improve the quality of life for individuals and communities by offering a wide range of services. Their efforts help tackle social issues and challenges within the community. These organisations depend on volunteers to carry out their work, and by volunteering, individuals can use their skills and time to make a difference in the lives of others, creating a positive impact in the community.

Volunteering also provides personal benefits, such as developing new skills, building social connections, and boosting self-confidence. In addition, contributing to a cause that matters can bring a sense of purpose and fulfilment, making the experience even more rewarding.

Giving back to the community.

Forms of Charities:

Numerous charitable and community organisations in the United Kingdom serve various causes and communities. Some of the common types of charitable and community organisations include:

1. Health charities: These charities work to improve the health and wellbeing of individuals and communities. Examples include Cancer Research UK, British Heart Foundation, and Macmillan Cancer Support.

2. Environmental charities: These charities work to protect the environment and promote sustainable living. Examples include Greenpeace UK, Friends of the Earth, and the Marine Conservation Society.
3. Social welfare charities: These charities work to address social issues such as poverty, homelessness, and unemployment. Examples include Shelter, Crisis, and the Trussell Trust.
4. Animal welfare charities: These charities work to protect and improve the lives of animals. Examples include the RSPCA, Dogs Trust, and the World Wildlife Fund.
5. Educational charities: These charities work to improve access to education and support learning. Examples include Teach First, the Sutton Trust, and the National Literacy Trust.
6. Arts and culture charities: These charities work to promote and support arts and culture. Examples include the British Museum, the Tate, and the Royal Shakespeare Company.

Contributing to Charities:

Getting engaged with charitable organisations is a form of service that can significantly influence both the lives of those being assisted and the volunteers. Every donation, whether volunteering time, contributing money or resources, or simply raising awareness, can have an impact. However, choosing to work with non-profit organisations can be a personal and difficult decision. It necessitates a willingness to step outside one's comfort zone, learn about many societal issues, and take significant action. In this regard, it is critical to understand the motivations for making this decision and how it fits with personal beliefs and ambitions. In this context, deciding to work with charitable organisations may be a rewarding and changing experience that benefits not just others but also the individual unexpectedly.

Depending on your interests, abilities, and availability, you can assist charitable organisations in various ways. Whatever you choose to do, your contribution can make a major difference in the lives of people in your communities and beyond. Some people engage in charitable acts of service in the following ways:

Donating:

Charitable organisations depend on contributions from both individuals and corporations to sustain their activities. These donations can take various forms, including monetary contributions, goods, or services. Such organisations rely on donations to finance their operations and provide support to those who require it. Donations can be earmarked for a specific cause or charity, such as backing research into a specific disease or aiding in providing clean drinking water in developing nations.

Donations can be made via various channels, such as online, over the phone, or in person. Some organisations also accept in-kind contributions, such as clothing, furniture, or food. Donating to charitable and community organisations in the United Kingdom is beneficial to those in need and can also offer tax benefits for the donor.

Volunteering:

Charities not only require financial assistance, but they also benefit significantly from volunteers' time and skills. Many organisations provide volunteer opportunities, allowing people to contribute actively. Volunteering, whether through event participation, administrative assistance, or professional skills, may be a satisfying opportunity for people to give back and make a big difference in the lives of others, even on a global scale.

Volunteering can be a rewarding experience that goes beyond selflessness. It offers an opportunity for personal growth. Through volunteering, we can meet new people, learn new skills, and gain valuable hands-on experience. By joining the many volunteers already making a difference, you can help create positive change in your community.

Fundraising:

There are many ways to contribute to charitable organisations through fundraising efforts. This can be achieved through efforts, such as organising events, taking part in sponsored walks or runs, or selling goods or services. Fundraising initiatives can be organised by individuals, groups, or organisations, and can vary in scale from small gatherings to grand galas.

Participating in fundraising events not only generates funds for charities but also raises awareness of their causes. These events can be an enjoyable way to engage with the community and build new connections.

Mentoring:

Voluntary and non-profit organisations often offer mentoring programs to support young people, disadvantaged individuals, or those facing challenges. By becoming a mentor, you can play a crucial role in providing guidance and assistance to those in need, thereby serving others through voluntary organisations in the United Kingdom. Mentoring can take many forms, such as giving young people career guidance and assisting those recovering from addiction.

Mentoring can take place either one-on-one or in group settings and is typically carried out by volunteers who desire to assist others and share their knowledge and expertise. By participating in mentoring, individuals benefit from the guidance and support they receive and, in the long run, can give back to their communities and develop valuable interpersonal skills.

Joining a Committee or Board:

If you possess business or leadership skills, you may want to consider joining the board of a community or voluntary organisation. Committees and boards include people with various backgrounds and skills, such as finance, marketing, or law. In this role, you can take an active part in shaping the organisation's direction, offering guidance and support to staff, and assisting with fundraising efforts. People who serve on committees and boards usually care deeply about the cause and want to make a difference. They are responsible for overseeing the organisation's day-to-day operations and ensuring that it achieves its objectives. Joining a committee or board of a charitable or community organisation in the United Kingdom allows you to make a difference and provides significant networking and leadership opportunities.

Finding a Charitable Organisation to Work With:

Whether your interest is in education, healthcare, the environment, or social justice, there is a charity out there working for the causes you care about. Supporting these organisations makes you an important part of the joint effort to address societal concerns. Individuals who want to volunteer their time or money must carefully consider which charities to support. It is critical to choose a cause consistent with your personal values, as this will have a significant impact.

Your Passion:

Before entering the world of charitable giving, take time to consider your passions and values. What causes tug at your heartstrings? Whether it's supporting children's education, providing shelter for the homeless, or preserving the environment, identifying your passion will guide you towards charities aligned with your personal values. Aside from your passions, think about what skills you have that you can offer to serve others. If you appreciate assisting children's education, consider volunteering as a school governor or in a local after-school programme. If you are a legal professional, you might want to consider donating your time to an organisation like the Citizens Advice Bureau.

Your Values:

Charitable organisations in the United Kingdom are diverse, ranging from small local initiatives to large national organisations. Each one operates with a unique mission and area of focus, addressing specific societal needs. If you want to give back through a charitable organisation effectively, aligning with causes that resonate with your values and interests is important. Consider examining key factors such as the organisation's mission, activities, and location.

Mission and Vision: Select an organisation that aligns with your values and interests by researching its mission and vision. Ensure that these align with the causes you wish to support.

Activities and Services: Check the organisation's activities and services to determine if they match your interests and skills. For example, if you are passionate about social justice, look into opportunities with such charities.

Impact: Evaluate the impact the organisation has on the community. Research their achievements and the outcomes of their activities to confirm they are making a positive difference.

Size and Location: Consider the size and location of the organisation. Larger organisations may have more resources and scope, whilst smaller ones may provide more opportunities for direct involvement. The location is also important, as it affects accessibility and the local impact of the organisation's initiatives.

Online Resources:

Finding and getting involved with charitable organisations is easier than ever before, thanks to the internet. By browsing online, you can explore the missions, activities, and impact of United Kingdom charities and gain insight into their aims and achievements. Websites like Charity Commission, JustGiving, and Charities Aid Foundation (CAF) provide valuable insights to help you make informed decisions. Additionally, global platforms like Idealist and VolunteerMatch connect individuals with organisations, including non-profits and social entrepreneurs, dedicated to creating positive change.

Local Engagement:

While national and international charities are important, do not underestimate the impact you could make in your own neighbourhood. Local charities frequently target specific needs in your surrounding area, providing a sense of belonging and community. Consider exploring local organisations or contacting community centres to find ways to contribute. Many non-profit organisations and community groups promote volunteer opportunities on social media platforms such as Facebook.

Contact the Identified Organisations:

Once you've found an organisation or group that interests you, contact them to learn about volunteer opportunities. When contacting the organisation, be clear about your abilities and interests and how you believe you can help them achieve their purpose. Ask about their volunteer opportunities and any requirements or skills required to volunteer. Many organisations will have an application process and may request a background check, particularly if you will be working with vulnerable populations such as children or the elderly. It is important to be patient throughout this process, as it may take some time to find the ideal volunteer position.

Commit to a Schedule:

Volunteering requires a commitment of time and effort. It is essential to communicate your availability and schedule with the organisation to determine the best times for volunteering. Depending on the organisation, volunteer schedules may be flexible or require a fixed commitment. It is important to be clear about your availability and commit to a schedule that works for both you and the organisation. It is essential to approach volunteer activities with a positive attitude and a willingness to learn and contribute. Be open to new experiences and challenges and take the opportunity to build relationships with other volunteers and members of the community.

Summary of Chapter 7
Charitable Organisations

- **The Role of Charitable Organisations**: Charities, such as Cancer Research UK and Save the Children, play a crucial role in tackling social issues like poverty, healthcare, and education. They rely on donations, grants, and volunteers to sustain their work.
- **Types of Charities**: Charitable organisations in the UK focus on different causes, including health, environmental protection, social welfare, animal rights, education, and arts and culture. Each type serves specific community needs.
- **Ways to Contribute**: Individuals can support charities through various means, such as donating money or resources, volunteering their time and skills, fundraising, mentoring, and joining charity boards or committees.
- **Choosing the Right Charity**: To make a meaningful impact, people should align their charitable contributions with their passions and values. Key considerations include the organisation's mission, activities, impact, and accessibility.
- **The Benefits of Involvement**: Engaging with charities not only benefits communities but also enables personal growth. Volunteering can build new skills, strengthen social connections, boost self-confidence, and provide a sense of purpose and fulfilment.

Chapter 8

The Church

One of the most influential servant leaders to ever walk the earth was Jesus Christ. His leadership was not defined by power, wealth, or political status but by humility, compassion, and a relentless commitment to serving others. Unlike rulers who sought to be served, Jesus washed the feet of His disciples, fed the hungry, healed the sick, and embraced the outcasts of society. His message of love, forgiveness, and selfless service transformed lives and continues to inspire millions around the world. The Church, as His body on Earth, carries forward this legacy of serving communities, guiding the lost, and standing as a beacon of hope. True leadership in the Church is not about titles or recognition; it is about serving with a heart of humility and a vision for transformation.

As a woman of faith, one scripture that deeply resonates with me is Acts 20:35, which emphasises the importance of giving rather than receiving. Whether or not you are religious, this mindset is crucial for being a person of value and serving others to the best of your ability. In this book, I've included this chapter on the church, not to exclude other religions, but because my own faith has given me a deeper understanding of its significance. My intention is to share insights from my experience that can inspire anyone, regardless of their faith, to embrace service and kindness.

The platform of a church provides a powerful space for individuals to engage in acts of service and contribute to the welfare of others. Selfless service is emphasised as a fundamental aspect of Christian living. By embracing the principle of serving others selflessly, individuals can fulfil the spirit of the

Bible's quote by embodying the selflessness and sacrificial love exemplified by Jesus Christ. Regardless of one's Christian denomination, one's local church or a house of worship may be a great place to find a welcoming community and compassionate individuals eager to assist those in need. Making a difference in people's lives through church participation can be fulfilling on various levels.

A place of worship and community.

There is the potential for the church platform to function as an opportunity for both individual and collective acts of service. To contribute their personal acts of service to the church community, individuals can make use of their skills and talents. This can be accomplished in various ways, including teaching Sunday school, mentoring young people, or providing support to those trying to overcome challenges. By doing so, a network of support is established, which contributes to an overall improvement in the congregation's well-being.

It's not uncommon for churches to organise gatherings where people can perform acts of kindness together. The church serves as the centre for various support groups and ministries designed to address specific needs within the congregation and the community. Individuals can use the church to begin acts of service by taking part in the church's many outreach programs and community service activities. These programs often address a wide range of needs, from feeding the hungry and providing shelter for the homeless to offering emotional support and companionship to the lonely and isolated. People can also use the church to make a difference in their communities by presenting educational events or organising fundraisers for worthy causes. These events not only benefit the community in practical ways but also strengthen the congregation's spirit and purpose.

The Heart of a Servant: Qualities of a Church Worker

Serving in the church goes beyond simply fulfilling duties; it requires a heart that seeks God's will and a spirit of humility. At its essence, being a church worker means following the example of Jesus Christ, the ultimate servant. The foundation of church service is rooted in love, which is love for God and love for others. A church worker should embody selflessness, patience, compassion, and other qualities aiming to uplift others rather than seeking personal recognition.

Selflessness: Serving in the church requires putting others' needs before one's own. True selflessness reflects Jesus' example of giving and caring without expecting anything in return. A church worker embodies this by willingly sacrificing time, effort, and personal desires to help others, showing a deep commitment to the church's mission and the well-being of its members.

Patience: Whether interacting with fellow workers or serving others, patience is vital. It allows church workers to serve others calmly, even when faced with difficult situations or challenging people. Patience is a virtue that enables one to bear burdens and handle setbacks gracefully, trusting that God's timing is perfect. This trait helps create a peaceful and supportive church environment where members feel valued and understood.

Compassion: A compassionate church worker actively seeks to understand and meet the needs of others, whether through prayer, emotional support, or practical assistance. This quality encourages a spirit of empathy and kindness, helping create a community where people feel genuinely cared for.

Love and Empathy: The core of service is rooted in love. A church worker's love for God and others drives their commitment to service. With love comes empathy, a deep understanding, and shared feeling with others' experiences. Love and empathy inspire a church worker to serve beyond what is expected, allowing them to connect with people's struggles and joys. This connection is essential for building a supportive, welcoming, and inclusive church family.

Humility: A humble heart allows a church worker to serve without pride or the need for personal recognition. It is a mindset of acknowledging God as the source of all strength and gifts, focusing on glorifying Him rather than seeking attention. This humility promotes unity and cooperation, as church workers understand that they are all servants of the same mission, working together for God's kingdom.

Faithfulness: A faithful church worker consistently serves with devotion, whether the task is large or small. This quality ensures that the church can rely on them, trusting that they will fulfil their duties with dedication and integrity. Faithfulness reflects a heart dedicated to God's service, regardless of external rewards.

A Teachable Spirit: A church worker should have a teachable spirit, always open to learning and growing in their faith. This quality reflects a willingness to listen, accept constructive feedback, and humbly seek ways to improve. A teachable spirit enables church workers to be moulded and guided by God, continuously evolving to serve more effectively.

Dependability: A dependable church worker honours their commitments, follows through on responsibilities, and supports their church family consistently. This trait builds trust and reliability, as the church knows they can count on their service, helping to strengthen the community and advance the church's mission.

Types of Service Roles in the Church

There are many ways to serve within the church, and each role is essential to building a strong, supportive community. While the role of a pastor or minister often requires an in-depth understanding of theology, there are numerous other ways for members of the congregation to contribute. I was ordained as a church elder, a role that calls for wisdom and the ability to provide pastoral care and support to fellow congregants. Ultimately, using your talents and skills, whether in a visible role or behind the scenes, helps advance the church's mission as an act of service. Some of the most common roles for serving in the church include:

Worship Team: If you have musical talents, whether playing instruments like the piano, keyboard, or guitar or if you enjoy singing, you might consider joining the choir. Worship teams play an important role in leading the congregation in praise and worship, helping to set a spiritual atmosphere for services.

Children's Ministry: Teaching and caring for young children during services is a deeply rewarding role. This ministry helps to lay the foundation of faith for future generations.

Ushering and Hospitality: Ushers and hospitality team members welcome visitors and regular attendees, helping them feel comfortable and valued. They are often the first point of contact for people entering the church.

Technical and Media Team: For those who are tech-savvy, this role involves managing sound systems, operating cameras, and ensuring online services run smoothly.

Prayer Team: If you have a heart for intercession, you can join the prayer team to pray for the needs of the congregation and community.

Administration and Organisation: Administrative roles involve helping with church logistics, organising events, and coordinating different ministry activities.

Interpreter and Sign Language: You can help bridge language gaps by translating sermons and services, making worship accessible to diverse groups.

Discovering Your Calling

Discovering where you fit in the church is a journey that requires both self-reflection and prayer. Here are some ways to discern where God might be calling you to serve:

Pray for Guidance: Seek God's guidance through prayer, asking for clarity and an open heart to His direction. Be patient and attentive, as His guidance may come through various means, such as scripture, advice from fellow believers, or personal conviction.

Reflect on Your Gifts and Talents: Think about the things you are naturally good at. Do you have a gift for teaching? Are you good with technology? Do you enjoy working with children? These abilities often reveal areas where you can make a meaningful impact. What activities bring you joy and a sense of purpose? Our call to serve often aligns with where we feel both capable and inspired.

Consider Your Life Experience: Your personal experiences, whether challenging or joyful, have shaped you and can be a source of strength for others. Reflect on how your background might help you connect with or serve others in the church.

Explore Different Ministries: Many churches have a range of ministries that rely on volunteers, such as children's programs, worship, outreach, hospitality, or teaching. Get involved in different areas to see what resonates with you and where you feel a sense of purpose.

Seek Advice from Church Leaders: Speak with your pastor or ministry leaders, as they may recognise gifts in you that you have not yet noticed. Talking with leaders or trusted mentors who understand your strengths and faith journey can provide valuable insights, guiding you towards roles that align with both your abilities and the needs of the church.

Start Small: You don't have to commit to a major role right away. Try different types of service to see what resonates with you. Volunteer at events, join a small ministry group, or assist in different areas.

Be Open to Growth and Change: Serving in the church is often a dynamic experience, and God may lead you to new roles over time. Stay open to evolving in your service, allowing room for growth, learning, and deeper connection with your faith.

Consider Your Availability: Be realistic about your time and energy. Start with a role that fits your schedule and commitments.

Preparing Yourself for Service

Before taking on any role, it's essential to prepare yourself spiritually, emotionally, and practically. Serving in the church is a rewarding experience, but it can also bring challenges. Here's how to equip yourself for this meaningful work:

Getting Ready Spiritually: Develop a strong spiritual foundation through prayer, scripture, and worship. Seek guidance from God to remain aligned with His purpose and lean on Him for strength and wisdom.

Emotional Readiness: Serving others can be demanding. Take time to reflect on your motivations and ensure that you're emotionally prepared for the journey. Building resilience through self-care and support networks can help you stay grounded.

Practical Skills: Certain church roles require specific skills or knowledge to be effective. For instance, if you're part of the media team, learning how to operate sound equipment is essential, while roles in children's ministry often involve training in child development and teaching techniques. Gaining these practical skills prepares you to serve well and enhances the overall ministry experience. Take time to learn your role: attend relevant training sessions, study resources, or seek mentorship.

Accountability: Having accountability is crucial to growing in any ministry. Surround yourself with mentors and fellow believers who can provide guidance, encouragement, and constructive feedback to help you stay on course.

Overcoming Challenges in Church Work

Church work can be incredibly fulfilling, but it is not without its difficulties. Some common challenges include burnout, interpersonal struggles, and feelings of inadequacy. Here are a few ways to overcome these challenges:

Avoiding Burnout: Burnout happens when you take on too much or when your work begins to overshadow your spiritual life. To prevent this, make time for rest and personal worship. Don't hesitate to step back and recharge when needed.

Dealing with Interpersonal Conflicts: Working closely with others can lead to misunderstandings or disagreements. Approach conflict with humility and a spirit of reconciliation. Pray for wisdom and strive to resolve disagreements in love.

Managing Feelings of Inadequacy: It's common to feel unqualified for your role. Remember that God doesn't call the qualified; He qualifies the called. Trust in His strength rather than your own abilities.

Balancing Church Service with Personal Life

One of the most challenging aspects of church work is balancing it with personal responsibilities. Here are some tips to help manage your time effectively:

Set Boundaries: Understand your limits. It's okay to say no if you feel overwhelmed. Setting clear boundaries will help you serve effectively without neglecting your family, work, or personal wellbeing.

Time Management: Prioritise your responsibilities and use tools like calendars or to-do lists to keep everything in balance. Dedicate specific times for church service, personal time with God, and family.

Involve Your Family: Where possible, include your family in church activities. This can make church service a shared experience, reducing the separation between your commitments and family time.

Service Beyond the Church Walls

True service extends beyond the walls of the church. As Jesus called us to be the light of the world (Matthew 5:14-16), our service should reach into the broader community. This means engaging in outreach programs, going on mission trips, or offering simple acts of kindness in our neighbourhoods. The impact of our service can stretch far beyond Sunday mornings. The Church of England, for example, is making a significant difference in communities across the UK through its various initiatives. From food banks to homeless shelters to supporting mental health services, the Church is actively working to meet the needs of those in need and positively impact society. These efforts show that serving others is not just a calling within the church but a vital part of building stronger, more compassionate communities.

Consider getting involved in various acts of service that can make a meaningful impact. Community outreach offers opportunities to volunteer at food banks, homeless shelters, or programs supporting the elderly and helping those in need. Evangelism allows you to share the gospel beyond the church walls, whether through organised missions or personal conversations, spreading hope and faith. Additionally, workplace ministry enables you to be a representative of Christ in your professional environment by embodying integrity, kindness, and grace in your daily interactions. Each of these avenues provides a unique way to serve others and contribute positively to society.

The Reward of Serving Faithfully

Serving faithfully in the church brings deep rewards, enriching both your spiritual life and personal journey. Jesus promises blessings to those who serve others (John 13:17). Through acts of service, your faith matures, your relationship with God strengthens, and you gain a renewed sense of purpose and fulfilment.

There is joy in seeing the impact of your efforts, whether it's a child learning about God's love, a person being comforted in prayer, or helping a soul draw closer to Christ. Above all, serving honours God and aligns your life with His will, leading to the ultimate reward: "Well done, good and faithful servant" (Matthew 25:23).

Spiritual Growth: As you serve, you find yourself drawn closer to God. Each act of service refines your character, strengthens your understanding of Scripture, and increases your reliance on God. This ongoing transformation deepens your faith and brings you into a more intimate walk with God.

Community and Fellowship: Service brings you into a community where fellowship thrives. As part of a church family, you experience a genuine sense of belonging, forming lasting relationships with others who share your passion for God and ministry. Together, you support each other's faith journeys, enriching both your life and theirs.

Eternal Impact: The work you do in God's name bears fruit that lasts beyond this life. Each time you help lead someone to Christ or sow seeds of faith, you contribute to an eternal legacy. In these moments, you're not only fulfilling God's call but making an impact that reaches into eternity, bearing fruit that endures.

SUMMARY OF CHAPTER 8
THE CHURCH

- **Servant Leadership in the Church** – Jesus Christ exemplified servant leadership through humility, compassion, and selfless service. The Church carries forward this legacy by serving communities, guiding the lost, and building transformation.
- **A Platform for Service and Community** – Churches provide opportunities for individuals to serve through teaching, mentoring, outreach programs, and community initiatives, promoting a network of support and well-being.
- **Qualities of a Church Worker** – Effective church workers embody selflessness, patience, compassion, love, humility, faithfulness, and a teachable spirit, ensuring they serve with integrity and a heart for others.
- **Diverse Service Roles in the Church** – From worship teams and children's ministry to technical support and hospitality, individuals can contribute their unique skills to advance the church's mission.
- **Service Beyond Church Walls** – True service extends into the broader community through outreach, missions, and acts of kindness, reinforcing the church's role in building a compassionate society.

Part Three

Serving The Nation

Chapter 9
Public Office

In 2017, the Grenfell Tower fire shook the United Kingdom to its core. Seventy-two lives were lost in a tragedy that exposed critical failures in housing policy, fire safety regulations, and government accountability. In the aftermath, public officials, local councillors, Members of Parliament, fire service leaders, and housing regulators were thrust into the spotlight, faced with urgent questions about responsibility and reform. Some stepped up to demand justice, while others worked tirelessly behind the scenes to ensure such a disaster would never happen again.

This tragedy was a stark reminder that public office is not just a title but a responsibility. Every decision those in power make affects real lives, often in ways that only become clear in moments of crisis. But beyond times of emergency, public officials are the cornerstone of public life, shaping policies that impact education, healthcare, justice, and economic development.

What is Public Office?

At its core, public office is about service. It is the trust placed in individuals to make decisions that promote the common good and uphold democratic values. In the United Kingdom, holding public office means taking on a role, whether elected or appointed, directly impacting communities, policies, and national governance.

Public office spans a vast range of sectors, including:

- **Government and Parliament** – MPs, councillors, and ministers who legislate and lead.
- **Judiciary and Law Enforcement** – Magistrates, judges, and police commissioners who uphold justice.
- **Education and Regulatory Bodies** – School governors, Ofsted inspectors, and policymakers who shape learning and social policies.
- **Public Health and Social Services** – NHS executives, local authority health officials, and social care directors who safeguard well-being.

Each of these roles contributes to the democratic framework that keeps society functioning. Without committed public servants, policies would lack direction, laws would go unenforced, and essential services would falter.

Who Holds Public Office?

Public office in the United Kingdom encompasses a wide range of roles, both elected and appointed, all dedicated to serving the public good. Elected officials include Members of Parliament (MPs), members of devolved parliaments and assemblies (such as the Scottish Parliament, Welsh Senedd, and Northern Ireland Assembly), local government councillors, mayors, and police and crime commissioners. Alongside them are appointed officials such as civil servants, judges, magistrates, and members of various government agencies and regulatory bodies. Each plays a vital role in upholding the principles of democracy, governance, and justice.

What Do Public Office Holders Do?

Public office holders have diverse responsibilities, depending on their specific roles. MPs represent their constituents, debate policies, and shape national laws. Local councillors oversee community services, from housing to education. Judges interpret and uphold the law, ensuring justice is served impartially. Regulatory bodies monitor industries to ensure compliance with laws and standards. Across all these roles, public office holders share a common duty: to make informed decisions, create policies, and implement services that enhance the lives of the people they serve.

Why Are Public Office Positions Important?

Public office positions are the backbone of a functioning democracy. They ensure that governance is transparent, accountable, and responsive to the needs of citizens. Public office holders shape policies, safeguard justice, and uphold the rule of law. Their work affects every aspect of daily life, from the economy and public safety to healthcare and education. Without dedicated individuals in these roles, the stability and progress of society would be at risk.

Where Do Public Office Holders Operate?

Public office holders serve at multiple levels of government, from the national stage to local communities. At Westminster, Parliament legislates on national issues, while devolved parliaments in Scotland, Wales, and Northern Ireland address regional matters. Local government officials operate in cities, towns, and villages, directly impacting community life. Judges preside over courts, civil servants work within government departments, and regulatory bodies oversee industries to maintain standards and fairness. Whether in a courtroom, council chamber, or government office, those in public service contribute to shaping the nation's future.

Motivations for Becoming a Public Office Holder

The decision to pursue public office is often rooted in a deep commitment to service, leadership, and the desire to create meaningful change. Public office holders play a crucial role in shaping policies, upholding democratic values, and ensuring the well-being of society. While motivations vary, they are often driven by civic responsibility, personal fulfilment, and the aspiration to leave a lasting impact.

Desire for Positive Change:

Many individuals step into public office because they are passionate about improving their communities and society at large. They see these roles as platforms for addressing pressing issues, championing reforms, and making a tangible difference in people's lives. Whether tackling social inequalities, improving public services, or driving policy innovation, these individuals are driven by a vision of progress.

Fulfilling Civic Duty:

For some, public service is more than a career; it is a duty. They recognise the importance of active participation in democracy and view holding office as a serious responsibility to represent and uplift their communities. This deep sense of obligation fuels their commitment to fair governance, accountability, and the protection of public interests.

Opportunity for Leadership:

Public office provides a unique opportunity for individuals to demonstrate leadership, influence decisions, and contribute to the governance of their country. Those with a strong sense of responsibility and governance find fulfilment in roles that allow them to shape policies, lead initiatives, and guide society towards a better future.

Advocating for Meaningful Causes:

Many public office holders enter their roles with a specific mission in mind—to advocate for causes they deeply care about. Whether it's social justice, environmental sustainability, economic growth, or public health, these individuals use their positions to amplify voices, push for legislative change, and drive impactful solutions at a systemic level.

Personal Fulfilment and Purpose:

Public office isn't just about making a difference in society; it can also be deeply rewarding personally. Serving others, solving important challenges, and helping communities thrive bring a strong sense of fulfilment. Knowing that their work impacts people's lives motivates public servants to stay dedicated to their roles.

Ethical Standards for Public Office Holders in the UK

For those currently serving or aspiring to public office, understanding the ethical responsibilities and standards of conduct is essential. Upholding integrity, accountability, and transparency is not just a requirement but a commitment to serving the public with honesty and dedication. Upholding the established guidelines helps public officials maintain trust and credibility while effectively fulfilling their duties.

One of the most fundamental frameworks governing public service ethics in the UK is the **Nolan Principles**, named after Lord Nolan, who chaired the Committee on Standards in Public Life. Established in 1995 in response to public scandals, these principles set the benchmark for ethical conduct in government and have since influenced private and voluntary sectors as well.

The Seven Nolan Principles

1. **Selflessness**: Public office holders should act solely in the public interest rather than for personal gain or advancement. They must set aside personal interests when making decisions.
2. **Integrity**: Individuals in public office must exhibit honesty, trustworthiness, and moral courage in all aspects of their conduct. Integrity requires avoiding conflicts of interest, being truthful and transparent in dealings, and upholding the highest ethical standards.
3. **Objectivity**: Public office holders should base their decisions and actions on evidence, reason, and impartiality without bias or favouritism. Objectivity ensures fairness and equality in the treatment of all individuals and groups within society.
4. **Accountability**: The principle of accountability requires public office holders to be accountable for their actions and decisions and to be transparent about how public resources are used. This includes being open to scrutiny and criticism and taking responsibility for any mistakes or failures.

5. **Openness**: Transparency is essential in maintaining public trust. Officials should be open about their decisions, actions, and the reasons behind them, ensuring that information is accessible to the public.
6. **Honesty**: Public office holders must be truthful and straightforward in their dealings, avoiding deception or withholding information relevant to the public interest.
7. **Leadership**: Those in public office should demonstrate leadership by promoting and upholding the highest standards of conduct and ethics. Leadership entails setting a positive example, inspiring others to act with integrity, and promoting a culture of ethical behaviour within public institutions.

Beyond the Nolan Principles, various codes of conduct provide specific ethical guidelines for different sectors within public service.

Civil Service Code: This code outlines the core values and standards of behaviour expected of civil servants in the United Kingdom. It emphasises impartiality, integrity, honesty, and accountability in delivering public services.

Ministerial Code: The Ministerial Code sets out the expected standards of conduct for government ministers. It covers issues such as conflicts of interest, relationships with lobbyists, and the importance of collective responsibility. Ministers are obligated to disclose any potential clashes of interest and to avoid situations where their personal interests could influence their decisions.

Local Government Code of Conduct: Local authorities in the United Kingdom operate under codes of conduct that set out standards for elected members and other officials, ensuring ethical and responsible governance. The codes cover various topics, including conflicts of interest, gifts and hospitality, use of resources, and relationships with the public.

Regulatory Codes: Different regulatory bodies oversee specific sectors, including finance, healthcare, and law. Professional bodies frequently establish codes of conduct to regulate the conduct of professionals in their respective fields. These codes aim to promote ethical behaviour and safeguard the public's interests.

By following these principles and codes, public office holders can maintain the public's trust, uphold democratic values, and serve with dedication and honour. Ethical leadership is the foundation of good governance, ensuring that public service remains noble and respected.

Answers to Common Questions on the Principles of Public Life

If you're looking to serve the public, embracing the Nolan Principles of Public Life is essential. These questions are a valuable tool for reflecting on your readiness to serve or for reinforcing the importance of these principles as you begin your public service journey. When answering, try to draw on real-life examples from your experience, showing how they align with the Nolan Principles. Share specific instances where you demonstrated these principles, explaining how they positively impacted your community or organisation. Additionally, consider any challenges you faced and how you navigated them while staying true to ethical standards. This reflection will help you recognise the significance of acting with integrity and affirm your commitment to serving ethically in your role.

Principle: Selflessness

Question: Can you provide an example of a time when you put the needs of the public or the organisation above your own personal interests?
Suggested Responses: Consider discussing instances where you went above and beyond your role to benefit others or the organisation without seeking personal gain.

Question: How do you ensure that your decisions and actions as a public servant are motivated solely by the best interests of the community you serve?
Suggested Responses: Highlight your commitment to transparency, integrity, and avoiding conflicts of interest.

Question: Describe a situation where you had to balance conflicting interests. How did you approach it?
Suggested Responses: Demonstrate your awareness of conflicts of interest and explain how you manage them. Discuss the steps you take to identify potential conflicts, disclose them, and make decisions that prioritise the public interest or the organisation's welfare over personal gain.

Principle: Integrity

Question: Describe a situation where you faced ethical dilemmas in your role. How did you uphold ethical standards and maintain public trust?
Suggested Responses: Emphasise your adherence to codes of conduct and ethical guidelines even in challenging circumstances.

Question: How do you demonstrate honesty and accountability in your interactions with colleagues, stakeholders, and the public?
Suggested Responses: Discuss your approach to transparency, truthfulness, and taking responsibility for your actions.

Principle: Objectivity

Question: Can you provide an example of a time when you set aside personal biases or preferences to make impartial decisions?
Suggested Responses: Illustrate your ability to weigh evidence objectively and consider diverse perspectives and evidence before making judgements.

Question: How do you ensure fairness and impartiality in your decision-making processes?
Suggested Responses: Talk about strategies such as consulting multiple sources, seeking input from diverse stakeholders, and applying consistent criteria.

Principle: Accountability

Question: Describe a situation where you took responsibility for a mistake or oversight in your work. How did you address it and prevent similar issues in the future?
Suggested Responses: Demonstrate your willingness to acknowledge errors, learn from them, and implement corrective measures.

Question: How do you hold yourself and others accountable for upholding standards of excellence and serving the public interest?
Suggested Responses: Highlight your commitment to performance evaluation, feedback mechanisms, and continuous improvement.

Question: How do you ensure the appropriate use of resources and public funds?
Suggested Responses: Describe your experience managing resources efficiently and responsibly, ensuring value for money. Highlight your strategies for budgeting, monitoring expenditures, and implementing effective controls to prevent misuse of public funds.

Question: How do you hold yourself and others accountable for ethical conduct and performance?
Suggested Responses: Discuss your approach to holding individuals accountable for ethical conduct and performance, including setting clear expectations, providing regular feedback, and implementing appropriate consequences for misconduct. Share examples of situations where you addressed ethical lapses effectively.

Principle: Openness

Question: Can you provide an example of how you promote transparency and openness in decision-making processes within your organisation or community?
Suggested Responses: Discuss initiatives such as public consultations, open forums, or accessible communication channels.

Question: How do you handle situations where there is a need for confidentiality while still upholding the principle of openness?
Suggested Responses: Share your approach to balancing transparency with the need to protect sensitive information or maintain privacy.

Question: How do you encourage feedback, input, and participation from diverse stakeholders in shaping policies and initiatives?
Suggested Responses: Describe your inclusive approach to governance, collaboration, and valuing diverse perspectives.

Principle: Honesty

Question: Describe a time when you communicated difficult or unfavourable information truthfully and tactfully.
Suggested Responses: Discuss your commitment to providing accurate and reliable information to the public.
Reflect on how you maintain credibility and trust through honest communication and actions.

Question: Describe how you maintain honesty and integrity in your interactions with colleagues, superiors, and the public.
Suggested Responses: Discuss any strategies you employ to maintain open communication and build trust.

Principle: Leadership

Question: How do you build public trust and confidence in your leadership?
Suggested Responses: Discuss your strategies for building trust and confidence among the public or stakeholders, such as open communication, delivering on commitments, and demonstrating accountability. Share examples of initiatives or projects where you successfully gained public trust.

Question: Describe a situation where you demonstrated leadership by promoting ethical behaviour and values among your peers or subordinates.

Suggested Responses: Showcase your ability to inspire others, set a positive example, and cultivate a culture of integrity and accountability within a team or organisation.

Question: How do you foster a culture of ethical leadership and public service within your team or organisation?
Suggested Responses: Discuss your role in promoting values, setting expectations, and fostering a supportive environment for ethical decision-making.

Question: Describe your approach to responsibly managing resources and assets entrusted to you.
Suggested Responses: Provide examples of initiatives you've implemented to promote sustainability and long-term viability. Discuss your commitment to leave a positive legacy for future generations through effective service.

Question: How do you promote the principles of meritocracy and equal opportunity in your leadership role?
Suggested Responses: Discuss your commitment to meritocracy and equal opportunity, outlining strategies you have implemented to ensure fair recruitment, advancement, and recognition based on qualifications and abilities rather than personal biases.

Question: Can you describe a situation where you have empowered others and developed future leaders in your organisation?
Suggested Responses: Share examples of how you have mentored, coached, or provided opportunities for growth and development to individuals within your team or organisation. Discuss how you have empowered others to take on leadership roles and contributed to their professional growth.

Summary of Chapter 9
Public Office

- **Public Office as a Responsibility:** The Grenfell Tower fire of 2017 highlighted the critical role of public officials in shaping policies that impact lives. Holding public office is not just a title but a responsibility to serve the public interest, ensure accountability, and make informed decisions.
- **Roles in Public Office:** Public office spans elected positions (MPs, councillors, mayors) and appointed roles (judges, magistrates, civil servants). These officials influence governance, justice, education, healthcare, and community services, ensuring policies are effectively implemented.
- **Motivations for Public Service:** Individuals pursue public office out of a desire for positive change, civic duty, leadership opportunities, advocacy for causes, and personal fulfilment. Their contributions drive reforms, uphold democratic values, and improve society.
- **Ethical Standards and the Nolan Principles:** Public office holders must adhere to ethical standards, including the Nolan Principles: selflessness, integrity, objectivity, accountability, openness, honesty, and leadership. These principles guide conduct, build trust, and ensure responsible governance.
- **Maintaining Public Trust and Transparency:** Effective public service relies on accountability, transparency, and ethical leadership. Codes of conduct, regulatory guidelines, and a commitment to ethical behaviour help officials uphold the public's trust and strengthen democracy.

CHAPTER 10

THE HOUSE OF LORDS

For decades, there were ongoing debates about the future of the House of Lords. Many argue that an unelected chamber has no place in a modern democracy, while others defend it as a necessary institution that provides expertise and scrutiny beyond the reach of party politics. It is one of the longest-standing political controversies in the United Kingdom. Nonetheless, the House of Lords continues to be one of the most important pillars of our democracy.

The House of Lords is the place where lords and baronesses are seated. This institution plays an important role in the United Kingdom Parliament, offering a unique opportunity for individuals to contribute to the nation's political framework. Functioning as the upper chamber alongside the elected House of Commons, it plays a vital role in shaping legislation and overseeing governmental actions.

Unlike the House of Commons, where members are elected, the House of Lords comprises appointed individuals selected by the Crown on the recommendation of the Prime Minister. This diverse assembly includes esteemed lords, baronesses, life peers, hereditary peers, and bishops, each bringing a wealth of experience and expertise to the legislative process.

Members of the House of Lords serve without a salary but are provided allowances to cover expenses such as travel and accommodation. Their service is rooted in a commitment to contribute to developing laws, scrutinising government actions, and providing invaluable insights into various policy areas.

Operating from the historic Palace of Westminster, where it convenes alongside the House of Commons, the House of Lords embodies a tradition of public service and civic engagement. Together, these chambers form the bedrock of the United Kingdom Parliament, working collaboratively to ensure effective governance and uphold democratic principles.

A Lord in the House of Lords

The Roles Played by Lords and Baronesses.

The House of Lords relies on the active participation of lords and baronesses to ensure the smooth functioning of the United Kingdom Parliament and the nation. As a vital part of the United Kingdom's legislative process, the House of Lords serves as a necessary check-and-balance mechanism. Their responsibilities, which include reviewing, revising, and scrutinising legislation, as well as holding the government accountable, are essential in maintaining the strength and integrity of the United Kingdom's democratic system.

1. Legislative Functions:

Legislative Review: The House of Lords reviews and revises bills (proposed laws) passed by the House of Commons. It scrutinises the details of legislation, suggests amendments, and ensures that laws are well-drafted and effective.

Delaying Legislation: The House of Lords has the power to delay the passage of legislation. It can propose amendments or send bills back to the House of Commons for further consideration. This delay provides an opportunity for a more thorough examination and debate.

2. Expertise and Experience:

Independent Expertise: The House of Lords consists of appointed members who bring expertise and experience from various fields such as law, business, academia, and public service. This diversity helps in ensuring a thorough analysis of proposed laws.

Long-Term Perspective: Unlike members of the House of Commons, who are elected for a fixed term, members of the House of Lords serve for life or until retirement. This allows them to take a long-term perspective on issues without being bound by short-term political considerations.

3. Checks and Balances:

Limiting Government Power: The House of Lords acts as a check on the power of the government and the House of Commons. It ensures that legislation is carefully considered and debated before becoming law. This helps prevent hasty or ill-conceived laws from being enacted.

Categories of Members of the House of Lords

The membership of the House of Lords is currently made up of a different group of individuals: hereditary peers, bishops, and life peers. Hereditary peers, whose titles have been passed down through generations, historically had significant influence, but their numbers have been reduced. The inclusion of bishops reflects the constitutional link between the church and the state. Most of the House comprises life peers, selected for their expertise and significant contributions to society. As of 2024, the House of Lords has 785 seats, with hereditary peers occupying 91, bishops 25, and life peers 669.

Hereditary Peers:

In the past, individuals born into noble families would inherit their titles and membership in the House of Lords as a matter of course. They primarily served as representatives of their titles and historical positions rather than being chosen based on specific expertise or accomplishments. One such example is Charles Spencer, brother of the late Princess Diana, a well-known figure in British society. He assumed the title of the 9th Earl Spencer upon his father's passing on 29 March 1992.

However, the House of Lords Act 1999 altered this tradition significantly. It substantially reduced the number of hereditary peers entitled to participate and vote in the House. Presently, only 91 hereditary peers remain, selected by their peers through an election process whenever vacancies arise. Among the noteworthy current hereditary members of the House of Lords is Edward Fitzalan-Howard, the 18th Duke of Norfolk. He is a prominent figure in British society and serves as Earl Marshal, overseeing state ceremonies like coronations and the State Opening of Parliament.

Bishops:

A group of twenty-five bishops from the Church of England, collectively referred to as the Lords Spiritual, are members of the House of Lords. The appointment of these bishops is completely automatic, and their primary objective is to ensure that religious perspectives are considered during the legislative process. There are guaranteed seats for the Archbishops of Canterbury and York, which are now held by Justin Welby and Stephen Cottrell, respectively. The appointments of the remaining bishops are made according to the length of service or experience they have had.

LIFE PEERS:

Life peers are individuals selected to join the House of Lords because of their outstanding achievements and significant contributions to society. The Crown makes appointments based on the prime minister's advice, following a process that will be explained in the next section. Those who are appointed are bestowed with the esteemed titles of Lord or Baroness. It should be noted that these titles are not inherited or passed down, though. They are only held by the individual for their lifetime and do not get transferred to their descendants.

These outstanding individuals bring a wealth of knowledge and experience to the House of Lords. Their backgrounds can cover politics, business, science, the arts, and more, making for a truly diverse and enriching House of Lords. Their commitment to serving the public and their determination to bring about positive change represents the noble principles on which the institution of life peerage is built.

For instance, Lord Victor Adebowale, elevated to the peerage in 2001, brings a wealth of experience in social entrepreneurship and mental health advocacy. His appointment recognises his pioneering efforts in bridging the gap between health services and marginalised communities, creating a more inclusive and compassionate society.

Similarly, Baroness Doreen Lawrence was appointed in 2013. Her tireless advocacy for justice following the tragic murder of her son, Stephen Lawrence, propelled her into the spotlight as a beacon for social change and reform. Her appointment to the House of Lords not only honours her personal resilience but also amplifies her voice in championing equality and combating racial injustice.

Then there's Lord Simon Woolley, whose appointment in 2019 reflects his groundbreaking work as a leading voice in race relations and community empowerment. As the founder of Operation Black Vote, he has been instrumental in mobilising underrepresented groups to engage in the political process, ensuring their voices are heard and their concerns addressed at the highest levels of government.

Path to Becoming a Life Peer in the House of Lords.

The selection of life peers is essential for maintaining the diversity and expertise within the House of Lords. Unlike hereditary peers, who inherit their titles, life peers are appointed based on their achievements, expertise, and contributions across various fields such as politics, business, academia, and public service.

Meritocracy is a key principle in the selection of life peers. The House of Lords Appointments Commission, an independent body established in 2000, ensures that appointments are merit-based, reflecting the diversity of society and bringing a broad range of experiences and expertise to parliamentary debates and decision-making.

The requirements for becoming a life peer in the House of Lords, the upper house of the United Kingdom Parliament, are as follows:

Eligibility	**Citizenship:** The individual must be a citizen of the United Kingdom, the Republic of Ireland, or a Commonwealth country.
	Age: The minimum age requirement is 21 years.
	Good Character: The individual must be of good character. This generally means having no serious criminal convictions or involvement in activities that would bring the House of Lords into disrepute.
	Financial Status: The individual must be financially solvent and should not have been declared bankrupt.
	Residency: The individual should be a resident of the United Kingdom for tax purposes.
	Political Disqualifications: • Members of the House of Commons cannot be appointed as life peers. • Certain public offices may disqualify an individual from being appointed (for instance, members of the judiciary while they hold office).

Nomination and Vetting	**Nomination:** Life peers are usually nominated by political parties, the Prime Minister, or through the non-political route by the House of Lords Appointments Commission. The appointment of life peers is formalised by the Crown, following the Prime Minister's or the Appointments Commission's advice.
	Appointments Commission: The House of Lords Appointments Commission vets all non-party-political nominations and can also make recommendations for non-political peers. They ensure that nominees meet the required standards of propriety.
	Prime Minister's Recommendation: Political appointments are often recommended by the Prime Minister, although they still undergo vetting.

NOMINATION PROCESS:

Life peers can be nominated by political parties, the Prime Minister, or through a non-political route by the House of Lords Appointments Commission. Some nominees are put forward by party leaders on a political basis, with their names submitted to the Prime Minister and then to the Crown for approval. Others, known as crossbench peers, are individuals with no party affiliation nominated by the independent Appointments Commission. This Commission aims to select individuals who bring independent thinking, expertise, and a commitment to public service to the House of Lords. Anyone can nominate a candidate to the Commission, and if they believe the person would make a significant contribution to the House, they can formally recommend them to the Prime Minister and the Crown for approval.

VETTING PROCESS:

The House of Lords Appointments Commission vets all non-party-political nominations and can recommend non-political peers. They ensure all nominees, including those recommended by the Prime Minister, meet the required standards of propriety. This rigorous vetting process scrutinises nominees' professional backgrounds, qualifications, ethical conduct, and potential conflicts of interest. The commission also assesses each candidate's ability to contribute effectively to the House of Lords and their commitment to its values and principles. Additionally, public consultation may be conducted, allowing stakeholders and the public to provide feedback on candidates' suitability for a peerage. This transparent approach helps maintain public trust and confidence in the integrity of the appointment process.

Appointment:

Based on their assessment, the Appointments Commission recommends a shortlist of candidates to the Prime Minister. The Prime Minister reviews the list and makes the final decision on who will be offered a life peerage. Once the decision is made, the Crown formally approves the selected individuals, granting them life peerages. Life peers receive membership in the House of Lords for their lifetime, and their titles typically include "Lord" or "Baroness."

Ceremonial Introduction

New life peers are introduced to the House of Lords through a formal ceremony. They take an oath or affirmation of allegiance to the Crown, acknowledging their duty to the House and the country. This ceremony marks their official entry into the House of Lords, allowing them to engage in the legislative process, attend debates, and contribute to the work of the House.

Summary of Chapter 10: The House of Lords

- **Role and Function**: The House of Lords, the upper chamber of the UK Parliament, plays a key role in reviewing and revising legislation, holding the government accountable, and providing expertise beyond party politics.
- **Membership and Structure**: Unlike the elected House of Commons, members of the House of Lords are appointed and include life peers, hereditary peers, and bishops. As of 2024, it has 785 members.
- **Legislative Impact**: The House of Lords scrutinises proposed laws, suggests amendments, and can delay legislation to ensure thorough debate and better lawmaking.
- **Checks and Balances**: It counterbalances government power by reviewing decisions, preventing rushed laws, and ensuring long-term national interests are considered.
- **Appointment of Life Peers**: Life peers are selected based on merit and expertise through nominations from political parties, the Prime Minister, or the independent House of Lords Appointments Commission, ensuring a diverse and knowledgeable membership.

CHAPTER 11

MEMBERS OF PARLIAMENT

Over the years, many people have asked why I haven't run for Member of Parliament (MP), especially after my years of service as a councillor and work in community development. Becoming an MP is often seen as the pinnacle of public service, a platform to shape laws, influence national policy, and directly impact the country's future. The role carries a significant responsibility, and the work MPs do is crucial for the well-being of society.

However, I've come to appreciate that service can make an impact in many different ways. Leadership isn't defined by your title but by the positive change you create wherever you are. Throughout my career, I've found purpose and fulfilment in my work with schools, the policies I've helped shape, and the communities I've served. These experiences have allowed me to make a difference, often in ways just as meaningful as those from a position in Parliament.

This chapter explores the world of Members of Parliament (MPs), their responsibilities, their impact, and their critical role in shaping laws and policies in the United Kingdom. While public office holds great power, it is the service itself that carries the greatest influence.

The United Kingdom Parliament is like a big house with two important rooms: the House of Commons and the House of Lords. In the House of Commons, we find Members of Parliament (MPs) elected to represent the people of the country. They make laws, speak up for their local areas, and keep an eye on what the government is doing.

The House of Lords, on the other hand, is different. It's not filled with elected politicians but rather a mixture of appointed members, including professionals in various sectors, such as science, law, or business, as well as hereditary peers who inherit their position. They use their knowledge to check and suggest changes to legislation proposed by the House of Commons.

Local councils are like smaller versions of Parliament. They focus on issues in specific areas, like cities or counties, while Parliament deals with big national matters. MPs often work closely with local councils to ensure that their constituents' concerns are heard at both levels of government.

So, whether it's in the House of Commons, the House of Lords, or through local councils, serving the nation is all about making sure that everyone's voice is heard and that laws are designed to benefit everyone.

The House of Commons

Members of Parliament (MP)

Members of Parliament (MPs) in the United Kingdom play a vital role in our democracy by representing and advocating for their specific constituency, which is one of 650 across the country. They are elected through a democratic process during parliamentary elections, ensuring every voice is heard and counted. As elected representatives, they prioritise accountability within the government, shaping the laws that govern our society and ensuring that every community is heard. By being a platform for their constituents, MPs provide a voice to the concerns of their respective areas and participate in national decision-making.

Serving as an MP is a noble act of service that requires a strong commitment to representing the people and communities they serve. Their service is more than just the opulence and ceremony of Westminster; it is about their practical impact on their constituents' lives. From addressing local issues to scrutinising government actions, MPs are the key players of democracy in action.

During their time in office, they strive to tackle governing challenges and fulfil their duties with honesty and dedication. Every five years, they willingly face the voters, offering to serve once again. For people who are passionate about politics and want to serve their community, becoming an MP is more than a job; it is a calling. It is about making a difference. The following provides more detailed information regarding the role of a Member of Parliament:

Representing their Constituents:

As an elected representative of their constituency, the main responsibility of a Member of Parliament (MP) is to serve as the voice and advocate of their constituency within the House of Commons. This involves actively engaging with and soliciting feedback from their constituents so that they can effectively represent their interests and concerns in Parliament.

To fulfil this role, MPs often hold regular advice surgeries with their constituents to listen to their views and address their questions and concerns. This provides constituents with a direct communication channel with their MP and allows them to seek guidance and support on matters affecting their lives.

In addition to being the voice of their constituency, MPs also play a crucial role in helping constituents access government services and programs. They may assist with issues related to healthcare, housing, employment, or immigration, among other things. MPs can provide guidance, advocate on behalf of their constituents, and liaise with relevant government agencies to ensure that their needs are being met.

Overall, a Member of Parliament must be responsive and accountable to their constituents, as they are the ultimate representatives of their community in the House of Commons. By actively listening to their constituents and providing them with the support they need, MPs can ensure that the concerns and interests of their community are properly represented in Parliament.

Making Laws:

In the United Kingdom, the process of creating laws is an important part of democracy, and MPs play a key role in it. They play an important role in developing laws that substantially impact the entire United Kingdom. They have the authority to introduce their own bills, which are proposed laws, as well as back and change bills introduced by the government (Prime Minister, Cabinet ministers, and civil servants responsible for running the country and implementing laws).

MPs are also appointed to committees that carefully scrutinise proposed legislation to ensure that the laws created are in the best interest of the country and their constituents. These committees play a critical role in the legislative process, as they conduct in-depth reviews of proposed legislation and recommend changes or improvements where necessary.

Holding the Government to Account:

MPs have an important role in holding the government accountable for its actions and decisions, promoting transparency and scrutiny within the democratic system. One key method used is asking questions and seeking clarifications from government ministers in the House of Commons.

During question time, MPs can directly question ministers about specific policies, actions, or decisions made by the government. This serves as a mechanism to scrutinise the government's actions, evaluate their effectiveness, and identify potential areas of concern. By raising these questions, MPs help ensure that the government remains answerable to the public and that decisions are made in the country's best interests.

Moreover, MPs have the power to hold the government accountable through debates on subjects of national importance. They can initiate discussions and deliberations in Parliament, bringing attention to pressing matters that require attention and action. These debates allow MPs to express differing viewpoints, challenge government policies, and offer alternative solutions. Through the exchange of ideas and arguments, MPs contribute to shaping public opinion and influencing government decisions.

Participating in Debates and Committees:

MPs participate in debates on various issues, including matters of national importance such as the economy, foreign policy, and social topics. During these debates, MPs can express their opinions, offer alternative solutions, and challenge the positions of other members of Parliament. By engaging in lively and informed discussions, MPs contribute to the development of new policies and legislation that reflect the interests and needs of the wider public.

Furthermore, MPs sit on committees that investigate and scrutinise the work of government departments. These committees are made up of MPs from different parties and have the power to conduct inquiries, gather evidence, and make recommendations to the government. For example, a committee may probe the government's response to an environmental issue, assess the impact of a new policy, or scrutinise the work of a specific government department. Through their participation in these committees, MPs ensure that the government remains accountable and transparent in its decision-making and that policies are based on robust evidence and analysis.

Representing their Political Party:

Being a member of a political party comes with a range of responsibilities, including the representation of the party's interests and policies within the Parliament. This entails that MPs align their voting patterns with their party's stance on crucial matters and collaborate with fellow party members to promote and advance the party's agenda.

When MPs join a political party, they become members of a larger group that shares common values, ideologies, and policy objectives. By abiding by the principles and goals of their party, MPs strive to present a unified front in Parliament. This unity facilitates effective decision-making processes and enables the party to work towards achieving its desired outcomes.

One prominent aspect of representing a political party in Parliament is the practice of voting along party lines. MPs generally coordinate with their party leadership and fellow party members to establish a consistent voting strategy on key issues. This means that when important legislative matters are being debated and voted upon, MPs typically cast their votes in accordance with the party's official position. By doing so, MPs showcase their commitment to the party's ideology and demonstrate a collective front, which can enhance the party's influence and effectiveness within the legislative body.

Building Relationships with other MPs:

Despite differing priorities and beliefs among political parties, MPs are elected to represent their constituents' interests and work for the betterment of their communities and the nation. Therefore, MPs sometimes need to set aside their ideological differences and work cooperatively with their peers from other parties to achieve common objectives.

Collaborating with MPs from other parties can bring many benefits, such as increased political influence, broader support for policies, and the ability to pass legislation that benefits a larger portion of the population. More so, the inclusive and collaborative political culture achieved by working together helps foster an environment where diverse perspectives are valued and considered.

Constituency Work:

In addition to their duties in Parliament, Members of Parliament (MPs) also play a vital role in serving their respective constituencies. They engage in various activities and initiatives aimed at improving the lives of the people they represent.

One of the most important aspects of constituency work involves meeting with local community groups and attending events to understand the concerns and needs of their constituents. By doing so, MPs can better represent their interests in Parliament and advocate for policies that address the unique challenges of their communities.

Furthermore, MPs also work to secure funding for local projects and initiatives, such as infrastructure improvements, education, healthcare programs, and job creation initiatives. They can also advocate for policy changes that support the growth and development of local businesses, which can improve the economic well-being of their constituents.

In general, constituency work is a critical aspect of an MP's job, as it allows them to build strong relationships with the people they represent and to work towards creating positive change in their communities.

Media Engagement:

MPs engage regularly with the media, conducting interviews, issuing statements, and engaging with the public through social media platforms. Being actively involved with the media is crucial for them, as they fulfil their responsibility of representing the public. Through active participation in these communication channels, MPs maintain transparency, accountability, and effective representation while building stronger connections with the communities they represent.

MPs often share their views on public issues, offering insights into legislative decisions, government policies, and current events. By speaking with journalists, they help to disseminate information and promote administrative transparency.

They also advocate for their constituents by amplifying their voices in the media, ensuring that their interests and concerns are recognised and addressed. Appearing on television and radio allows them to reach a larger audience and deliver important messages.

In recent years, social media has become an essential tool for MPs to communicate directly with constituents and the public. Platforms such as X (formally Twitter) and Facebook allow MPs to share updates, address queries, and engage in conversations, resulting in a more inclusive political process.

How to Become a Member of Parliament

As previously pointed out, being a member of the UK Parliament is a highly regarded position that allows one to have a big impact on people's lives across the country. It is a tough yet rewarding endeavour that requires a combination of skills, competence, and dedication. The process of becoming an MP is a difficult endeavour that requires hard work, devotion, and a strong sense of civic duty. You can either run as an independent candidate or join a political party that shares your values; this allows you to participate in political activities, get experience, obtain party endorsement, campaign, and ultimately run for office.

Choosing a Political Party

It is common for MPs to have affiliations with political parties, as the typical route to becoming an MP involves being selected as a candidate by a political party. In the UK, various political parties exist, such as the Conservative

Party, the Labour Party, the Liberal Democrats, and the Scottish National Party (SNP). It is important to consider your values, principles, and policy preferences when deciding which political party to support. As a member, you would be required to participate in party events and actively interact with party members to develop a comprehensive understanding. Being a party member typically requires payment of a membership fee and following the party's constitution and rules.

Selection Process – Parliamentary Candidate

The selection procedure for becoming an MP may vary slightly depending on the political party. Ideally, individuals selected to run for election in a certain constituency would have been party members for a significant period, contributing to party activities and rising through the ranks. The actual selection process can be rigorous, involving interviews and ballots by constituency party members. Here is an overview of the steps you can expect:

- Connect with your local constituency party to demonstrate your interest in becoming a candidate. Make sure to attend meetings and campaign events and get to know party members and supporters in your area.
- Every political party has its own selection process. Participating in the process typically requires completing an application, engaging in interviews, and effectively communicating your position to local party members. It is crucial to demonstrate your commitment, leadership qualities, and understanding of local and national issues.
- The party will carefully assess potential candidates and conduct a selection process, including interviews by a panel of members, a hustings event where you can deliver speeches, and a ballot by party members. If you are successful, you will be selected as the official candidate for your party in the constituency.

Requirements for Running as a Candidate in the Parliamentary Elections

In addition to meeting the criteria for becoming a successful candidate for the political party, there are other requirements for being officially nominated to run in the parliamentary election. To become a candidate in an upcoming parliamentary general election, you must first secure a valid nomination. This involves completing a nomination form, which must be endorsed by ten electors from the constituency, referred to as subscribers. Additionally, a £500 deposit is required to validate your nomination.

Below is a summary of the requirements. It is worth mentioning that the process may vary slightly depending on the specific election regulations and procedures at the time. For precise guidance, it is advisable to consult the Electoral Commission or the relevant local authority.

Eligibility	Citizenship: You must be at least 18 years old, a British citizen, a citizen of the Republic of Ireland, or a citizen of a Commonwealth country with the right to live in the United Kingdom.
	Age: You must be at least 18 years old to stand for election.
	Disqualifications: Certain individuals, such as civil servants, members of the armed forces, and judges, are disqualified from becoming MPs. Furthermore, bankrupt individuals, prisoners serving a sentence of more than one year, and individuals convicted of corrupt practices are also ineligible.
Political Party or Independent Candidate?	If a political party selects you as their candidate, you are eligible to run as their candidate. Alternatively, you can run as an independent candidate with no party connection.
Nomination Papers	You must complete a set of nomination papers the Returning Officer issues for the constituency where you intend to run. This normally includes your name, address, and, if applicable, political affiliation, as well as the name and contact information of your nominated election agent. They must also acknowledge their responsibilities and sign your papers.
Pay a Deposit	Candidates are normally required to make a deposit, which is repaid if they receive a particular proportion of the vote in the election. The deposit is intended to dissuade frivolous candidates.

Provide Details for the Ballot Paper	You need to provide details for the ballot paper, including how you would like to be identified.
Consent to Nomination	You must sign a consent form confirming that you agree to run for election.

Election Campaigning

Once your nomination is accepted, you can begin campaigning. This involves promoting your policies and persuading voters to support you. Your activities include canvassing voters, attending debates, giving speeches, and promoting your campaign through social media and other channels. It's imperative to engage with voters and listen to their concerns and priorities. A successful campaign requires a strong message, effective communication skills, and a dedicated team of supporters.

- Develop a comprehensive campaign strategy with the assistance of your party's campaign team. This may include identifying key issues, organising public meetings, canvassing door-to-door, and utilising social media.
- Engage with voters by attending local events, debates, and public forums. Establish a strong connection with constituents by listening to their concerns and articulating your policies effectively. Candidates often participate in hustings and debates, where they can present their views and engage with voters.
- Ensure your campaign receives funding through appropriate sources such as party support and personal contributions. It is crucial to have a clear understanding of the regulations regarding election spending and donations and to adhere to them. You and your election agent must comply with all election rules and regulations, including spending limits and reporting requirements.

Election and Post-Election Process

On the day of the election, the voters in your constituency will vote to choose a Member of Parliament. The candidate with the most votes will become the

MP for that constituency. Before sitting in the House of Commons, you must take an oath of allegiance. As a new MP, you will undergo an induction program to learn about parliamentary procedures, rules, and ethical guidelines. Your primary role as an MP will be to represent and champion the concerns and needs of your constituents. This will involve holding regular advice surgeries, engaging with local organisations, and participating in debates and discussions in Parliament.

Useful Links for UK Parliamentary Candidates

Running for an elected position in the UK Parliament requires substantial time, effort, and financial resources. It is highly beneficial for candidates to seek information, guidance, and advice from diverse organisations dedicated to promoting democracy, offering supportive services, and providing electoral resources. Please note that the list provided below is not exhaustive, as there may be other organisations that could be helpful for individuals interested in pursuing a career as an MP.

1. The Political Studies Association (PSA) - https://www.psa.ac.uk - The PSA is an organisation that promotes the study of politics and political science in the UK. They offer a range of resources and support for people interested in politics and public service. Contact them at: info@psa.ac.uk.
2. The Electoral Commission - https://www.electoralcommission.org.uk/ The Electoral Commission is an independent body that oversees elections in the UK. They provide guidance on the legal requirements for running as an MP, including how to register as a candidate and how to comply with campaign finance rules.
3. The UK Parliament - https://www.parliament.uk/ The UK Parliament is the legislative body of the UK government. Their website provides information on the roles and responsibilities of MPs and guidance on how to become an MP.
4. The House of Commons Library - https://commonslibrary.parliament.uk/ The House of Commons Library provides research and

analysis on various issues for MPs. Their website is a useful resource for anyone looking to learn more about the policy areas in which MPs are involved.

5. The Hansard Society - https://www.hansardsociety.org.uk/ - The Hansard Society is an independent, non-partisan organisation promoting democratic engagement and political literacy in the UK. They offer a range of resources, events, and training for people interested in politics. Contact them at info@hansardsociety.org.uk.
6. Unlock Democracy - https://www.unlockdemocracy.org.uk/ Unlock Democracy is a campaign organisation promoting democratic reform, transparency, and citizen engagement. They offer resources, training, and support for candidates advocating for democratic changes, including electoral reform, lobbying regulations, and accountability. Contact: info@unlockdemocracy.org.uk
7. Democratic Audit UK https://www.democraticaudit.com/ Democratic Audit UK is an independent research organisation focusing on democracy, election integrity, and political participation. They provide analysis, reports, and evaluations of the state of democracy in the UK, offering valuable insights for candidates aiming to improve democratic processes and public trust. Contact: info@democraticaudit.com
8. The Conservative Party - https://www.conservatives.com/ - The Conservative Party is one of the UK's major political parties. They offer support and resources for people interested in becoming Conservative MPs. Contact them at office@conservatives.com.
9. The Labour Party - https://labour.org.uk/ - The Labour Party is another major political party in the UK. They offer support and resources for people interested in becoming Labour MPs. Contact them at info@labour.org.uk.
10. The Liberal Democrats - https://www.libdems.org.uk/ - The Liberal Democrats are a political party supporting liberal policies and values. They offer support and resources for people interested in becoming Liberal Democrat MPs. Contact them at info@libdems.org.uk.

11. The Green Party - https://www.greenparty.org.uk/ - The Green Party is a political party that advocates for environmentalism and social justice. They offer support and resources for people interested in becoming Green Party MPs. Contact them at info@greenparty.org.uk.
12. The Scottish National Party (SNP) - https://www.snp.org/ The Scottish National Party is a political party in Scotland that advocates for Scottish independence. If you are interested in becoming an SNP MP, their website provides information on the selection process and how to get involved in the party.
13. The Plaid Cymru - https://www.partyof.wales/ Plaid Cymru is a political party in Wales that advocates for Welsh independence. If you are interested in becoming a Plaid Cymru MP, their website provides information on the selection process and how to get involved in the party.

Summary of Chapter 11
Members of Parliament

- **Role and Responsibilities of MPs** – Members of Parliament (MPs) represent their constituencies, advocate for their concerns, and shape laws in the UK. Their duties include participating in debates, holding the government accountable, and engaging in constituency work.
- **Law-Making and Governance** – MPs help draft, debate, and pass legislation. They serve on committees to scrutinise proposed laws and policies, ensuring they align with national interests and benefit their constituents.
- **Holding the Government Accountable** – MPs question government ministers, participate in debates, and challenge policies to ensure transparency and good governance and that decisions reflect the needs of the public.
- **Path to Becoming an MP** – Individuals can become MPs by joining a political party, engaging in local politics, and being selected as a parliamentary candidate. Independent candidates can also run but must meet eligibility requirements, including securing nominations.
- **Public Engagement and Media Presence** – MPs communicate with the public through media interviews, social media, and community meetings. They use these platforms to advocate for their constituents, raise awareness of key issues, and influence public opinion.

Chapter 12

Local Government

Standing for election as a local government councillor was both exciting and daunting. Would my message appeal to the voters? Would they trust me to represent their needs and concerns? These were the questions I carried with me as I campaigned, going door to door, speaking with residents, and listening to their concerns. Elections are unpredictable, and no matter how much you prepare, the ultimate decision is in the hands of the voters.

When I was elected for the first time, it was an incredible honour. To be entrusted with representing people and making decisions that directly impact their daily lives was both empowering and humbling. But I quickly learned that public service isn't just about being in office; it's about how you use your position and power to make a meaningful difference.

During my 16 years as a councillor, I worked hard to support my constituents, tackling difficult local issues and helping to shape council policies. Housing shortages, youth services, and community safety were just some of the pressing concerns that needed attention. Finding solutions required determination, collaboration, and a constant focus on what would truly benefit the people I represented.

Being elected four times was a testament to the trust my community placed in me. Each election brought its own challenges, but it also reinforced my commitment to serving. The local media later described me as a "formidable campaigner," a title I earned by successfully winning four elections, even against strong opposition from groups like the British National Party (BNP) and the National Front. These experiences strengthened my dedication to public service and deepened my belief in the importance of strong leadership to drive positive change.

One of the biggest lessons I learned in office was that service requires both patience and boldness. It means standing firm in your convictions while being willing to listen and adapt. It means making hard decisions that may not please everyone but always keeping the people's best interests at heart.

Looking back, I realise that every challenge, late-night meeting, difficult decision, and victory was part of a greater purpose. Public service isn't easy, but when done with integrity and commitment, it is one of the most powerful ways to bring about real change. My time as a councillor deepened my understanding of governance and reaffirmed my belief that one person can truly make a difference in their community.

Councillors play an important role in advancing democratic values at the local level by serving as a vital link between the people and the local authority. England alone has around 17,000 councillors serving on 317 local authorities. Each area has its own distinct form of local administration. There are county and district councils, unitary authorities, metropolitan districts, and London boroughs.

Councillors are usually elected to serve a four-year term, with the possibility of seeking re-election. Their main duty is to improve their local communities by providing essential public services. This involves overseeing a range of services the local council offers, including housing, education, transportation, social services, and environmental management. In addition to allocating resources and approving budgets, councillors are responsible for ensuring that public funds are used efficiently to meet the community's needs.

Elected councillors have an important responsibility in representing the people they serve and advocating for their needs. This involves supporting policies that address local concerns and priorities. They are required to actively participate in council meetings, serve on committees, and collaborate with stakeholders to enhance the wellbeing of their constituents and achieve positive changes at the local level. Below is a summary of the primary functions of councillors:

Policy Making and Decision-Making

Councillors are supposed to participate in policymaking procedures in their respective councils. They design policies and strategies to meet the needs and priorities of their constituents. Councillors also make decisions about the budget, service delivery, and planning applications.

Representing their Wards

Councillors are elected to represent a specific geographic area known as an electoral ward. Advocating for the interests and concerns of the ward residents is one of their primary responsibilities. They serve as a link between the local community and the council, advocating for people's needs and ensuring that their views are heard in decision-making processes. This could include attending meetings, communicating with constituents, and responding to requests and complaints.

Community Engagement and Outreach

Councillors engage with local communities to obtain feedback, provide information, and encourage civic participation, especially during election periods. They attend community events, hold advice surgeries, or arrange appointments with constituents to air their concerns and explain council decisions and objectives to the general public. Councillors must be accessible and approachable. Councillors can build relationships, promote transparency, and foster civic participation by engaging in outreach.

Scrutiny and Oversight

It is important for council members to closely examine the decisions and actions made by the council to ensure transparency and accountability. Councillors take part in committees that oversee and scrutinise council performance, services, and policies. They keep the council accountable for its actions and find areas for improvement by conducting inquiries, questioning senior council officers, and reviewing reports.

Community Development and Support

Council members support community development programs designed to improve residents' living standards. This might include connecting with local organisations, supporting community projects, and campaigning for resources to address youth provision, infrastructure, and social care.

Legislative Compliance and Governance

Council members must operate in accordance with the laws and regulations that control their local government operations. They are responsible for ensuring that the council follows all relevant laws, regulations, and procedures. As representatives of the electorate, council members are responsible for always acting with honesty and integrity and maintaining the highest ethical standards in their work.

Collaborative Working

Councillors collaborate with one another, council staff, and other stakeholders to achieve shared goals and objectives. They engage in cross-party discussions, joint initiatives, and partnerships with neighbouring authorities, community groups, and government agencies such as the police and NHS to address common issues like crime prevention and public health. Councillors work to address complex topics and provide effective services to their communities by encouraging cooperation and consensus-building.

Casework

Councillors assist residents with various concerns and inquiries, such as housing problems, benefit claims, and local disputes, by liaising with the council's relevant departments, agencies, and authorities. Furthermore, councillors also offer support and guidance to constituents who need help accessing local services and resources.

Civic Duties

Councillors actively participate in various civic ceremonies, events, and celebrations, reflecting the spirit of local government and promoting civic pride. These ceremonies cover multiple occasions, including the annual Remembrance Day services held in honour of veterans and the Mayor Making ceremony, which marks the transfer of duties to new civic leaders. By participating in these events, councillors become respected ambassadors of their communities, creating positive impressions of the area and building strong relationships with external stakeholders.

A Town Hall – The heart of civic leadership.

How to Become a Councillor

If you are interested in positively impacting your community and advocating for residents, consider becoming a local government councillor in the UK. Much like becoming a Member of Parliament (MP), becoming a councillor involves a similar commitment to public service and community representation. Both roles require individuals dedicated to serving their constituents and influencing decisions that shape the community's future.

As a councillor, you have the power to influence decisions made by your local authority and represent the interests of your constituents, much like an MP does at a national level. To be effective in either role, you should have a passion for public service and a strong desire to make a difference in your community or country.

Additionally, both councillors and MPs need excellent communication and interpersonal skills. They must articulate their constituents' needs and concerns effectively and collaborate with colleagues to achieve common goals. Whether at the local or national level, the ability to work with others and build consensus is crucial for success in public office.

Join a Political Party or Stand as an Independent Candidate:

If becoming a councillor interests you, there are ways to approach it. One option is to align yourself with a political party and work your way up through the ranks. It is important to be well-informed about the political parties active in your area and find the one that most closely aligns with your core beliefs and values. Alternatively, you can run as an independent candidate, which allows you to remain unaffiliated with any political party. Regardless of your choice, being an active and informed member of your community is crucial to make a positive impact as a councillor.

Selection Process – Councillor Candidate

The process of selecting candidates for local elections varies among different political groups, each with its own unique procedures and criteria. However, political parties frequently employ highly competitive methods in their candidate selection. Within these parties, members and local leaders play pivotal roles in vetting and endorsing candidates, ensuring their alignment with party principles and the community's needs.

Typically, candidates undergo a thorough vetting process, which may involve submitting applications, attending interviews, and undergoing background checks. Potential candidates often participate in public forums or debates organised by the party, allowing party officials and local members to hear their speeches and responses to questions. Community involvement, agreement with party objectives, and the ability to win elections are all important considerations.

Requirements for Running as a Candidate in Local Elections

You are expected to meet certain qualifying requirements and follow due processes to stand as a candidate in the local elections. The information you need about the requirements can be obtained from your political party or the relevant local authority. Below are the broad requirements that must be met:

Eligibility	**Citizenship:** You must be a British citizen, a citizen of the Republic of Ireland, or a Commonwealth citizen who is eligible to vote.
	Age: You must be at least 18 years old to stand for election.
	Voter Register: You need to be registered to vote in the area or have lived, worked, or owned property there for at least 12 months before an election.
	Disqualifications: Certain individuals are ineligible to run for local elections. These include civil servants, employees of the specific local authority where they seek candidacy, or individuals holding politically restricted positions in another local authority. Additionally, undischarged bankrupts are also disqualified.
Nomination Process	You have two options for nomination: either a registered political party can nominate you, or you can nominate yourself as an independent candidate. To proceed, you'll need to fill out a nomination form, providing essential details like your name, address, and political affiliation, if applicable. This process involves securing a proposer, a seconder, and assentors. In total, you'll require endorsement from 10 individuals listed on the electoral register of the ward where you intend to run.
Ballot Paper	You need to provide details for the ballot paper, including how you would like to be identified.
Consent	You must sign a consent form confirming that you agree to run for election.

Local Election Campaigning

Once you secure your nomination as an election candidate, planning an effective campaign strategy becomes necessary. This includes developing various outreach approaches to engage constituents effectively and establish yourself. If you are representing a party, you can expect support from your party, which may include campaign materials and volunteers to help with leaflet distribution, door-to-door canvassing, and voter turnout.

Here is a breakdown of campaign methods that may be useful for any type of campaign, whether in local or general elections:

1. Prioritise Community Engagement Through Various Channels:

Engaging with the community is of utmost importance for any candidate. Prioritising community engagement through various channels can help you connect with constituents, understand their concerns, and showcase your dedication to addressing their needs.

Consider attending community events such as fairs, markets, and gatherings to meet with people and learn more about local concerns. Implementing door-to-door canvassing efforts can also be effective in gaining insight into constituents' issues and cultivating trust through direct interaction. These approaches demonstrate your commitment to the community and foster a deeper understanding of local problems, ultimately strengthening your candidacy.

Furthermore, you can seize the opportunity to build your database of supporters by asking if they would like to provide their mobile numbers for further communication or follow-up. Remember to obtain their consent to comply with GDPR laws.

2. Effectively Use Digital Platforms:

It is recommended that you join social media platforms such as Facebook, Twitter, and the Nextdoor app to establish an online profile and communicate with your neighbourhood. Many communities now have dedicated Facebook groups where you interact with voters by reacting to their comments and postings. You can also hold live sessions to keep people engaged and share your thoughts. This method will allow you to communicate with constituents and rally their support for your candidacy.

3. Facilitate a Campaign or Petition Addressing Crucial Local Issues:

One effective strategy for uniting the community and addressing its problems is to promote campaigns and conversations on local issues. By creating a welcoming space for individuals to share their thoughts and ideas, you can empower residents and show that you value their opinions. As a result, you can establish a positive reputation as someone eager to take the lead and committed to working collaboratively with the community to achieve positive change.

4. Connect with Local Media:

It is important to connect with your local media to publicise your campaign message effectively. You should be open to having interviews with media outlets such as your local newspapers and community radio stations. Building relationships with them can help you showcase your commitment to serving the community and keep people updated on your campaign. These platforms provide a great opportunity to share your goals and plans with a large audience and let them know what you stand for.

Election Day and Beyond

Polling stations generally open their doors at 7 a.m. and close them at 10 p.m., providing ample opportunity for eligible voters to exercise their democratic rights. For those who choose postal voting, ballots are sent out approximately two weeks prior to Election Day, allowing voters to mail them back at their convenience.

On Election Day, candidates can engage in door-to-door campaigning to increase voter turnout and convert undecided voters. This is the final phase of a comprehensive campaign aimed at securing the votes required for victory. Additionally, candidates may visit polling stations briefly to observe proceedings and enhance their visibility among voters.

Vote verification and counting commence after the polling stations close, with election officials overseeing the collection and tallying of ballot papers. The counting typically takes place in a venue capable of accommodating all relevant parties. Candidates, their guests, party members, and counting or election agents are usually present during the count.

Following the completion of vote counting, the results are announced, either late on Election Day or in the subsequent days, depending on the scale of the election and the efficiency of the counting process.

For a newly elected Councillor, signing the declaration of acceptance of office is a momentous occasion. It signifies your commitment to fulfilling the duties entrusted to you by your constituents.

Common Questions for Political Candidates

If you want to be an MP or councillor, you should prepare for candidate selection screenings and media interviews opportunities. Some important concepts for political leaders to understand include their policy views, leadership skills, and public engagement. With this understanding, you may approach interviews with confidence, answering questions intelligently, eloquently, and with integrity.

Question	Possible Response
What inspired you to become involved in politics?	Interviewers want to know how driven and passionate you are about serving the public. Your response can focus on the significance of supporting the party's agenda, promoting certain policies or values, or helping the community. "I have always been passionate about making a positive impact in my community and helping others. I firmly

	believe politics is a potent means for achieving those goals."
What is your vision for the country, and how does your party's platform reflect that vision?	Interviewers are interested in understanding your political ideology and how it aligns with your party's agenda. A possible response could be: "I envision a society that is fair and equitable, where everyone has access to opportunities regardless of their background. Our party's platform reflects this vision by focusing on key issues, including education, healthcare, and social welfare."
What do you think are the biggest issues facing your constituency right now?	Your understanding of local concerns and your ability to address them are being explored. Potential response: "I have been talking to residents and organisations in my constituency about several issues, including a shortage of affordable housing, access to healthcare, and boosting the local economy. I strongly believe that investing in these vital areas will make a meaningful difference in the lives of our constituents, and I will continue to fight for increased funding to make this a reality."
How do you plan to engage with your constituents and stay connected to their needs and concerns?	Interviewers are trying to assess your communication skills and commitment to engaging with the public. You can respond by saying, "My plan is to hold regular public meetings, visit local businesses and organisations, and pay close attention to the concerns of my constituents. I firmly believe that effective representation requires excellent communication.
How do you plan to balance the needs of your constituents with the priorities of your political party?	Interviewers are interested in understanding how you handle conflicting priorities between your constituents and your political party, a situation that can arise in politics. A suitable response could be: "I am committed to prioritising the needs of my constituents above all else. While I value the principles of my political party, my foremost responsibility is to represent the interests and concerns of the people who elected me."
What sets you apart from the other candidates in this race?	The interviewers are interested in finding out what makes you stand out. To come up with your response, think about using your personal experiences, accomplishments, or qualifications. You might, for example, assert, "I bring a new perspective to politics thanks to my varied background, which includes working in the private sector and being an active member of my community. I will stop at nothing to resolve the problems that affect our community.

How do you plan to work with members of other parties to achieve your goals?	Interviewers are interested in understanding your ability to work well with others and build strong alliances. A suitable response could be: "I firmly believe in the importance of seeking common ground across party lines to drive progress on matters significant to our constituents. I am committed to working with individuals who share a common goal of creating a brighter future for our communities.
How do you plan to address social inequality in your constituency?	Interviewers want to know how well you understand and are committed to addressing social and economic inequalities. The answer could focus on policies concerning education, housing, or employment. For example, "I believe we need to invest in education and job training programs and raise the minimum wage to help lift people out of poverty. I also support progressive taxation and other policies that promote greater economic equality."
What is your position on climate change and environmental policy?	Interviewers are seeking to assess your position on a critical global issue and your plans for addressing it. The answer might focus on renewable energy, reducing carbon emissions, or encouraging environmentally friendly practices. For example, "I believe that climate change is one of the most pressing issues we face today. I support investments in renewable energy, sustainable transportation, and policies to reduce carbon emissions and protect our natural resources."
What is your stance on immigration, and how does your party plan to address this issue?	Interviewers want to hear your opinions on immigration and how you intend to address the associated difficulties. The answer could centre on policies affecting asylum seekers, refugees, and economic migrants. For example, "I believe that immigration is essential to our country's success and prosperity." My party intends to develop a fair and equitable immigration system that is both practical and compassionate."
What steps will you take to promote economic growth and job creation in your community?	Interviewers want to learn how you plan to strengthen the local economy and create employment. The answer could focus on building infrastructure, tax incentives, or support for small businesses.
What are your views on public health policy?	Interviewers want to hear your views on healthcare policy and how you intend to help improve access to care. The answer could include funding for the National Health Service (NHS), improving primary care, or reducing waiting times.

How do you plan to actively promote diversity and inclusion within our communities?	Interviewers are interested in understanding your level of commitment to diversity, equity, and inclusion. It would be useful if you could emphasise your passion for connecting with diverse communities, promoting respect, understanding of various cultures, and keenness for policies tackling discrimination. An example response could be, "I strongly believe that a diverse and inclusive society is essential for our country's success. I am committed to working with my party and other stakeholders to promote diversity and inclusion in all areas of society."
What measures will you take to promote transparency and accountability in your work as an elected official?	Interviewers are interested in understanding your dedication to maintaining transparency and accountability in public office. The public is interested in understanding your strategy for promoting transparency in decision-making and upholding ethical standards. Some potential approaches could involve pushing for legislation that promotes transparency, communicating with constituents regularly, supporting independent regulatory bodies, and promoting a culture of integrity.
What are your thoughts on education reform?	Interviewers are interested in hearing your ideas for improving the education system and equipping young people for the future. Your response could focus on areas such as funding, curriculum development, or teacher training. For instance, one could express the belief that education is crucial for achieving success, emphasising the importance of investing in schools and educators. Creating a fair education system that provides equal opportunities to all learners, regardless of their socio-economic background, is of top priority.
How do you plan to address the issue of homelessness and housing affordability in your constituency or the country as a whole?	Interviewers want to know how you plan to address homelessness and housing affordability. They want to understand your strategies for dealing with this pressing issue, either at a local level or nationally. Possible responses include advocating for an increased affordable housing supply, supporting homelessness prevention programs, and collaborating with local authorities and housing organisations to implement effective solutions.
What is your position on national security and defence and how do you believe the UK should protect its citizens and interests?	Interviewers are interested in gaining insight into your perspective on national security and defence and how you prioritise the protection of citizens and national interests. They want to assess your knowledge of security challenges and possible strategies to tackle them. One possible approach is to advocate for increased defence spending,

	ensuring that our alliances remain strong, and investing in intelligence capabilities to effectively address emerging threats. It is important to prioritise diplomatic solutions alongside these measures.
Why are you interested in becoming a councillor, and what motivates you to serve your local community?	Interviewers want to know why you want to be a councillor and how committed you are to helping the community. They want to understand your motivations and values. Possible responses include a desire to make a positive impact, address community needs, and participate in local decision-making processes, all driven by a love for public service and community improvement.
What do you think is the role of a councillor?	Interviewers want to know how well you understand the function of a councillor and how committed you are to public service. They aim to assess your understanding of local government responsibilities and engagement with the community. Possible answers involve representing constituent interests, developing local policies, scrutinising council decisions, and working with stakeholders to successfully address community needs, resulting in a vibrant and thriving community.
What skills do you have that would make you an effective councillor, and how would you use these skills in your role?	Through probing questions about your relevant skills and potential contributions, including your ability to successfully address community concerns, interviewers hope to determine your suitability for the role of councillor. Strong communication skills for engaging constituents, problem-solving abilities to address local concerns, analytical skills for evaluating policy options, and interpersonal skills to work with fellow councillors to implement solutions that benefit the community. These are some suggestions you could consider.
What experience do you have in working with local communities, and how would you apply this experience to your role as a councillor?	Interviewers seek to understand your community engagement skills, which will be useful in your work as a councillor. They want to see how conversant you are with local issues and how you can engage with constituents. Previous involvement in community organisations, local initiatives, or volunteering efforts that demonstrate a dedication to understanding and addressing the issues of local communities may form part of your response.
How do you plan to engage with the local community?	Interviewers want to know how you intend to engage in the community and interact with your constituents once you become a councillor. The approach you choose to address their issues and concerns, develop relationships, and

	involve residents in decision-making. Some possible responses include displaying your ability to promote discussion, such as having councillor advise surgeries, organising public meetings as needed, establishing community forums, and participating in local events.
What are the biggest challenges facing your ward, and how would you address them if elected?	The interviewers aim to assess your familiarity with your electoral ward and your plans to address local concerns effectively. Demonstrating awareness of key issues impacting the ward illustrates your commitment to serving as a councillor and your readiness to tackle local challenges. For instance, if anti-social behaviour is a concern, you could propose collaborating with police for community policing and increasing youth engagement programs in collaboration with local authority officers and community organisations.
How would you ensure that public services are delivered effectively to residents?	Interviewers are interested in learning about what you do to ensure that residents receive public services efficiently. Responses can include emphasising transparency, obtaining resident feedback, and scrutinising relevant council departments to ensure resources are prioritised and service quality is enhanced. Establishing accountability measures to ensure that public services meet expectations and that community complaints are effectively handled.
How would you ensure that your decisions as a councillor are transparent and accountable to residents?	Interviewers want to understand your commitment to transparency and accountability. They want to know your approach to balancing transparency in decision-making with integrity. There are a few potential responses to the question, such as using an independent oversight committee to scrutinise the council's activities and spending and promoting the open disclosure of performance data. Creating newsletters to communicate council decisions effectively. Regularly participating in community forums to fully engage residents and using social media platforms to collect valuable feedback and suggestions.
What is your vision for your borough if you are elected as a councillor, and how would you work to make it happen?	The interviewers want to know how well you understand the borough's needs and how you plan to address them effectively. Express a clear vision for improved infrastructure, community engagement, and sustainable development. Emphasise collaborative efforts with residents, businesses, and local organisations. Highlight your commitment to transparency, accountability, and inclusivity in decision-making processes. Ensure efficient use of resources and continuous evaluation of progress.

How would you address issues around access to healthcare in your borough?	Interviewers want to know how well you understand the healthcare access concerns in your borough and how you intend to address them. You may respond by highlighting the importance of community health clinics, increased funding for public healthcare services, forming partnerships with local organisations to provide outreach programs, and advocating for policies prioritising equitable healthcare access for all residents.
In response to residents' concerns about antisocial behaviour and crime, how would you make your ward and borough a safer place to live?	Interviewers want to assess your approach to community safety and your ability to address residents' concerns effectively. Highlight initiatives like increased community policing, neighbourhood watch programs, improved street lighting, and partnerships with local organisations for youth engagement. Emphasise the importance of collaborative efforts between residents, law enforcement, and local authorities to address underlying causes of antisocial behaviour and crime.
How would you engage with young people and ensure that their voices are heard in local decision-making?	The interviewers want to understand how you would engage young people and incorporate their viewpoints into local decision-making. Emphasise creating inclusive platforms, such as youth councils or forums, facilitating their direct involvement. Encourage participation through social media outreach, community events, and workshops based on the young people's interests. Prioritise active listening and respecting their opinions to develop their sense of belonging and ownership in local government initiatives.
How would you work with other councillors and stakeholders to achieve your goals?	To check your capacity to collaborate effectively, interviewers look at your interpersonal skills, leadership, and ability to work with councillors of different political backgrounds to reach a common goal. Emphasise your commitment to open communication, active listening, and being ready to find a point of agreement. Highlight past experiences of successful teamwork and your approach to engaging diverse perspectives. Express willingness to engage stakeholders, including local businesses and community groups, to facilitate productive discussion and achieve goals.
How would you support local businesses and help to boost the local economy?	Interviewers want to know how committed you are to the local economy and supporting local businesses. You can discuss your ideas for boosting local businesses, such as encouraging entrepreneurship and improving access to resources like grants and training. It's important to show

	you care about keeping the community strong and ensuring the economy grows in a way that's good for everyone. For instance, you may discuss plans to encourage local spending by implementing discount programs, raising awareness about community events, and promoting business networking opportunities.

Useful Links for Councillors

Exploring resources from organisations focused on local government can provide valuable insights into council operations, helping you understand a councillor's responsibilities and how to address key community issues.

1. Local Government Association (LGA) - https://www.local.gov.uk/ - The LGA represents local authorities in England and Wales, providing guidance, training, and support for councillors. Their website offers resources on governance, policy, and best practices.
2. National Association of Local Councils (NALC) - https://www.nalc.gov.uk/ - NALC represents town and parish councils in England, offering guidance and support to councillors at the grassroots level. Their website includes resources on governance, community engagement, and training opportunities.
3. The website of each local council will offer information on the election process, local issues, and services. These websites typically provide contact information for council officers who can offer assistance and guidance.
4. Electoral Commission - https://www.electoralcommission.org.uk/ - The Electoral Commission is responsible for administrating and regulating elections in the UK. Their website provides information on electoral law, campaign finance rules, and electoral registration.
5. Association for Public Service Excellence (APSE) - https://www.apse.org.uk/ - APSE is a membership organisation that supports local government in delivering high-quality services. They offer resources, events, and training programs focused on various aspects of local government.

6. Media: Local newspapers, radio stations, and internet news platforms frequently cover local elections and provide information about local issues and concerns. They can give publicity for your campaign, enable you to communicate your message to the public, and create awareness about local concerns.
7. Local political parties: If you belong to a political party, your party's local branch or constituency office can give campaign support and resources, as well as connect you with experienced campaigners and councillors who can offer advice and guidance.
8. Local community and interest groups: Communicating with local community organisations, residents' associations, and interest groups in your constituency can help you understand local issues and generate support for your campaign.

Summary of Chapter 12
Local Government

- **Election Experience**: Standing for local government elections is both exciting and daunting, with the ultimate decision resting in the hands of the voters. It's a chance to represent community needs and make a real difference through public service.
- **Lessons from Service**: Serving as a councillor requires both patience and boldness. It involves tackling local issues, making tough decisions, and being a voice for the community, all while maintaining integrity and focus on the greater good.
- **Councillor Responsibilities**: Councillors play a vital role in local governance, from policy-making and budget decisions to community engagement and oversight. Their work impacts public services like housing, education, and community safety.
- **How to Become a Councillor**: Aspiring councillors must meet eligibility criteria, join a political party or run as independents, and undergo a competitive selection process. Campaign strategies include community engagement, digital outreach, and local media connection.
- **Election Day and Post-Election**: On Election Day, candidates work to boost voter turnout, with campaigns continuing through door-to-door visits and media interaction. Results are tallied, and newly elected councillors sign the declaration of acceptance to begin their service.

Part Four

Essential Institutions

CHAPTER 13

THE JUSTICE SYSTEM

In 1998, through my work in community development at Southwark Council, I played a role in monitoring the Operation Black Vote (OBV) campaign led by Simon Woolley, now Lord Woolley. OBV aimed to empower Black and ethnic minorities to engage in civic life and take on leadership roles across Britain. During this time, I was introduced to the idea of becoming a magistrate, a role I had never previously considered. The thought of serving in the judiciary fascinated me, and I decided to pursue it and submitted my application in 1999.

The application process was rigorous, involving multiple stages before my name could be forwarded to the Lord Chancellor for appointment. It demanded dedication, the ability to make fair and balanced decisions, and a deep commitment to justice. In 2002, I was sworn in at Southwark Crown Court as a Justice of the Peace, marking the beginning of my journey in the magistracy. This was followed by extensive training through the Judicial College to prepare me for the responsibilities ahead. A role that would allow me to serve my community in a profoundly impactful way.

I have truly enjoyed serving in this capacity and have proudly contributed over 20 years to the magistracy. Along the way, I have mentored countless new magistrates, helping to guide and support those stepping into this vital role. My dedication to the judiciary led me to become a Presiding Justice, ensuring fair hearings and upholding the principles of justice. It has been an honour to serve, knowing that every decision made contributes to a fairer society.

Magistrates

Serving as a magistrate in the UK offers a unique and impactful way to engage in public service within the judiciary. Magistrates, also known as Justices of the Peace, play a crucial role in maintaining law and order by handling a significant portion of criminal and civil court cases. This role is accessible to a diverse range of individuals and provides an opportunity to contribute meaningfully to the justice system, uphold the rule of law, and make a positive difference in the community.

Magistrates are lay judges who volunteer their time to serve in magistrates' courts across England and Wales. Unlike professional judges, magistrates do not need formal legal qualifications. Instead, they receive specific training to equip them with the necessary skills and knowledge for their duties. Typically, magistrates sit in panels of three, with one acting as the presiding justice or chairperson, and make decisions collectively.

Magistrates' courts handle a wide range of cases, including minor criminal offences, family matters, and some civil disputes. Their jurisdiction covers summary offences (less serious crimes) and either-way offences (crimes that can be tried either summarily or on indictment). Magistrates also conduct preliminary hearings for more serious offences before they are referred to the Crown Court.

The Role of Magistrates in Justice

The contribution of magistrates to the justice system is invaluable. By dealing with a substantial volume of cases, they alleviate the burden on higher courts, ensuring that the judicial system functions efficiently. Magistrates bring local knowledge and community perspectives to their decision-making, which enhances the relevance and acceptance of their judgements.

While serving as a magistrate is rewarding, it comes with its challenges. Magistrates must balance their judicial responsibilities with their personal and professional lives. They are required to commit to a minimum of 13 days of service per year, plus training days, which can be demanding for those with busy schedules.

Decision-making in the magistrates' court can be complex and, at times, emotionally taxing, especially in cases involving vulnerable individuals or sensitive issues. However, the opportunity to make a tangible difference in the community and contribute to upholding the rule of law is a significant reward for many magistrates.

How to Become a Magistrate

Applying to become a magistrate is a significant commitment that involves a rigorous selection process and a comprehensive training program. While the time it takes to complete the process can vary, it is generally estimated to take up to 12 months from application to appointment. By understanding the eligibility criteria, completing the application form diligently, and preparing for the interviews and assessments, you can increase your chances of being appointed as a magistrate and embarking on a fulfilling journey of serving the community and contributing to the administration of justice.

Eligibility Criteria for Magistrates

The process of becoming a magistrate is open to a wide segment of the population, demonstrating the judiciary's commitment to diversity and community representation. To apply to become a magistrate in the UK, applicants must meet certain eligibility criteria, ensuring they possess the necessary qualities and skills to fulfil their responsibilities effectively. The general requirements for becoming a magistrate are as follows:

Eligibility	**Citizenship:** British nationality is not a requirement, but you must be willing to take the oath of allegiance to the Crown. Those with indefinite leave to remain in the UK can apply.
	Age: You must be at least 18 years old, and usually, not older than 70 as magistrates must retire at 75. They are normally expected to serve for at least 5 years.
	Disqualifications: A criminal record or certain serious offences may disqualify an individual from becoming a magistrate.

Excluded Professions:	Individuals with certain jobs or professions are automatically disqualified from applying to be magistrates. Police officers, probation officers, or prison officers are among those who cannot serve as magistrates. These disqualifications ensure that magistrates preserve their impartiality and the court system's integrity.
Skills and Qualities:	While no formal legal qualifications are required, you should possess certain key skills and qualities, such as sound judgement, good communication skills, social awareness, maturity, fairness, commitment, and the ability to work well as part of a team.
Character and Health:	Applicants are expected to have good character and integrity, as well as good physical and mental health.
Selection Process	The selection process involves several stages, including an application form, interviews, and assessments to evaluate the candidate's suitability. The Lord Chancellor then appoints successful candidates on behalf of the Crown. New magistrates undergo comprehensive training provided by the Judicial College, which covers courtroom procedures, legal principles, and practical skills.

The Application Journey

Before applying, it is crucial to familiarise yourself with the responsibilities of a magistrate and assess your suitability for the role. A wealth of information is available online, particularly at magistrates.judiciary.uk, where you can find more up-to-date information and guidance notes. Ensure that your current employment does not affect your eligibility. Consider the time commitment, responsibilities, and potential challenges to determine if this role aligns with your interests and availability.

Court Visits and Observations:

It is a mandatory requirement that you make at least two visits to magistrates' court to observe court proceedings within 12 months prior to your application. Observing magistrates in action in the court is an important prerequisite that offers a valuable opportunity to understand court procedures and assess whether the role suits your interests and abilities. The experience will also help you prepare for the interview if selected. You can visit any magistrates' court in England and Wales.

During your observations, ensure you see various cases, such as summary trials, guilty pleas, bail applications, and other hearings. It would be good if you identified yourself as a prospective magistrate upon arriving at the court so that you might be directed to the appropriate courtroom. Pay attention to the interactions between magistrates, court officials, legal professionals, and defendants. This experience will deepen your understanding of the role and strengthen your application.

If you are applying to be a magistrate in the Family Court, where cases are not open to the public, you will need to research the role instead of court observations.

Application Process:

Once you have completed your court visits and are confident in pursuing a magistrate position, you can begin the application process. The Ministry of Justice provides detailed guidance notes for applicants, which should be carefully reviewed before proceeding. The application process typically involves the following steps:

Online Application:

Complete the online application form, providing accurate and comprehensive information about your personal details, qualifications, employment history, and reasons for wanting to become a magistrate. Before submitting your application, obtain the consent of your referees. You must provide contact details for three referees who have known you for at least three years, with one referee being your current employer if you are employed.

Review of Application:

After submitting your application, it will be reviewed by the Recruitment Advisory Committee responsible for your area. They will assess your eligibility and suitability based on the information provided in the application.

Qualifying Assessment and Interview:

If your application is selected for further consideration, you will receive an invitation to participate in the magistrate recruitment qualifying assessment. Upon successful completion of the assessment, you will then be invited to attend an interview (either remotely via MS Teams or in person). These assessment and interview stages are designed to evaluate various aspects, including your aptitude, comprehension of the role, and capacity to make fair, unbiased judgements. The process may involve situational judgement tests, scenario-based inquiries, and discussions centred around legal and ethical matters.

References and Checks:

Following the interview, the Ministry of Justice will conduct a Disclosure and Barring Service (DBS) check. The DBS check ensures that individuals with a history of certain offences are not appointed as magistrates.

Appointment:

If you successfully pass all stages of the application process, you will be recommended for public appointment to the judiciary as a magistrate. The Lord Chancellor makes the appointment based on the Advisory Committee's recommendations.

Swearing-in Ceremony:

Once appointed, you will be required to attend a swearing-in ceremony. During this ceremony, you will take an oath or affirmation to perform your duties faithfully and impartially as a magistrate. This ceremony is usually conducted in a formal setting, such as a courtroom, and may be attended by other magistrates, court officials, and local community members.

Training and Support:

As a new magistrate, you will undergo comprehensive induction training to equip you with the necessary knowledge and skills. This training covers both theoretical and practical aspects of administering justice, ensuring you understand the legal framework within which magistrates operate and are proficient in courtroom management and decision-making processes. Once you have completed your induction training, you can begin sitting in court.

Furthermore, beyond the initial training, magistrates continue to receive ongoing development to stay updated on legal changes and refine their skills. Continuous professional development ensures magistrates remain effective and fair in their judicial duties.

Mentorship is also a vital part of a magistrate's development. For the first 12-18 months, newly appointed magistrates receive ongoing support and guidance from an experienced magistrate on their bench, ensuring a smooth transition into their duties.

Possible Interview Questions and Responses

This section provides a collection of general and scenario-based questions along with suggested responses based on my practical experience in magistrates' work. This resource is intended to assist you in your decision to become a magistrate, including the application and interview preparation.

The questions and responses are quite broad and should not be taken as actual interview questions. They do, however, provide more in-depth insights into the six fundamental traits required for success as a magistrate: good character, understanding and communication, social awareness, maturity and sound temperament, sound judgement, and commitment and reliability. The scenario-based questions may also help you comprehend the proceedings in magistrate courts.

Questions About "Good Character"

Magistrates must have personal integrity, be circumspect and able to maintain confidences and have nothing in their private or working life or the lives of their family, close relatives, or close friends that could bring them or the magistracy into disrepute.

Questions	Suggested Responses
As a magistrate, personal integrity is critical. Can you give an example of a time in your personal or professional life when you displayed integrity, and how this relates to your potential role as a magistrate?	Share an example from your personal or professional life that demonstrated your commitment to integrity. For example, you may discuss a situation where you were faced with a moral dilemma and chose to act in an honest and principled manner, even when it was difficult or inconvenient. Emphasise how this commitment to integrity would carry over into your role as a magistrate, where you would be entrusted with upholding the law and making fair judgements.
Maintaining confidence is an important aspect of being a magistrate. How have you demonstrated circumspection and the ability to keep information confidential in your previous roles or personal life?	Provide examples of situations where you were entrusted with confidential information and successfully maintained confidentiality. This could include scenarios from your professional experience or instances where you were a confidant for a friend or family member. Emphasise your understanding of the importance of confidentiality in the judiciary, as well as your dedication to protecting it as a magistrate.
The requirement for magistrates to have good character extends to their private lives as well as those of their families, close friends, and relatives. Can you assure us that nothing in your private life or the lives of your family and close friends could potentially bring disrepute to the magistracy?	Offer a clear and concise response confirming that there is nothing in your private life, the lives of your family members, or close friends that could potentially compromise the integrity and reputation of the magistracy. You could mention that you have always been mindful of your actions and have surrounded yourself with individuals who share the same commitment to upholding high ethical standards. Stress that you understand the importance of maintaining a strong reputation both inside and outside the courtroom.
How would you handle a situation where you become aware that a family member, close relative, or close friend has engaged in behaviour that may bring disrepute to the magistracy?	In your response, explain how you would approach such a situation with integrity and professionalism. Emphasise that you would immediately distance yourself from any activities or behaviour that could reflect negatively on the magistracy. You would also prioritise the values of the judicial system over personal relationships, ensuring that your decisions on the bench remain unbiased and objective. It is important that you highlight your commitment to upholding the integrity of the magistracy, even if it means making

	difficult choices or confronting challenging situations.
Can you provide examples of how you actively separate your personal and professional life to ensure that one does not affect the other?	Share specific strategies to separate your personal and professional life. For instance, you could mention that you have a strong sense of boundaries and understand the importance of not allowing personal matters to interfere with your duties as a magistrate. Discuss any organisational or time management techniques you use to avoid conflicts of interest or distractions. You can demonstrate your commitment to maintaining the magistracy's integrity by showing your capacity to separate and stay focused on your judicial duties.

Questions Regarding "Understanding and Communication"

Magistrates must be able to communicate effectively with colleagues, court users, and court staff; be able to comprehend relevant facts reasonably quickly; follow evidence and arguments, and concentrate, often for long periods.

Questions	Suggested Responses
Can you provide an example of a situation where you have effectively recognised and appreciated different perspectives? How did you demonstrate understanding and empathy towards those involved?	In your response, be sure to provide a specific example from your personal or professional life where you experience an issue with multiple views. Describe how you actively listened to each viewpoint, acknowledged the validity of their concerns, and displayed empathy by considering their individual circumstances. Highlight any steps you made to bridge gaps or find common ground between the various viewpoints.
How do you ensure effective communication when dealing with individuals from diverse backgrounds or who have different levels of understanding?	In your response, emphasise the importance of clear and respectful communication. Discuss techniques you have used to adapt your communication style to suit the needs of different individuals. Mention how you have utilised active listening skills, avoided assumptions or biases, and explained complex concepts in accessible language. Emphasise your ability to establish rapport and create a safe

	and non-judgemental space for open communication.
Magistrates often must concentrate for long periods during court proceedings. Can you provide an example of a situation where you demonstrated strong focus and sustained attention?	Describe a situation where you had to focus fully for an extended period. Share your methods for managing distractions, staying focused, and successfully completing tasks or achieving desired outcomes. Discuss the strategies you plan to use during hearings, including active listening, asking clarifying questions, and note-taking.
Give an example of a time when you had to comprehend complex arguments or evidence and follow them accurately.	Describe a situation where you encountered complex arguments or evidence, either in a professional or personal context. Explain how you approached the information, broke it down into manageable components, and ensured you fully understood the key points. Discuss your ability to critically analyse information, ask relevant questions, and apply logical reasoning to follow the arguments accurately.
Effective communication extends to interactions with court staff. How would you ensure respectful and constructive communication with court personnel?	Describe your approach to building positive working relationships with colleagues and court staff. Highlight your ability to listen attentively, acknowledge their expertise, and treat them respectfully and professionally.

Questions Regarding "Social Awareness"

Magistrates must appreciate and accept the need for the rule of law in society; display an understanding of wider social issues, such as the causes and effects of crime; have respect for, and some understanding (to be developed through training) of, people from different ethnic, cultural or social backgrounds.

Questions	**Suggested Responses**
How do you demonstrate your appreciation for the rule of law?	Demonstrate your awareness of the role of the rule of law in preserving a just and orderly society. You can express your commitment to the law, respect for legal processes, and belief in the principles of fairness and equality before the law. You might also talk about any previous experiences or involvement in legal or community activities that have strengthened your respect for the rule of law.

Can you provide an example of a social issue related to the causes and effects of crime that you are aware of and how it impacts the community?	Discuss a social issue that demonstrates your awareness of the broader context surrounding criminal behaviour. One example of a social issue related to the causes and effects of crime is the prevalence of drug addiction. Substance abuse not only affects individuals and their families but also has wider effects on the public. Drug-related crimes often stem from addiction, and they can contribute to increased rates of violence, property offences, and strain on healthcare and social services.
How would you handle a case involving individuals from a cultural background different from your own?	You can emphasise your ability to approach cases with an open mind, free from prejudice or stereotypes. You can discuss the importance of cultural competence, which involves understanding and respecting the beliefs, values, and traditions of different cultures. You should express your willingness to seek guidance when needed, use interpreters if language barriers exist, and ensure that the proceedings are fair and inclusive for all parties involved.
How would you ensure that your decisions as a magistrate are fair and unbiased, considering the diverse backgrounds of those who may come before you in court?	Mention that to ensure fair and unbiased decisions, you would actively seek to overcome any unconscious biases by engaging in self-reflection and ongoing training. You would make a conscious effort to treat everyone who comes before you in court as an individual, regardless of their background. You would carefully consider the facts of each case, examine the evidence presented, and apply the law impartially. You can mention that your goal would be to ensure that justice is served fairly and equitably for all individuals, regardless of their ethnic, cultural, or social background.
How do you stay informed about social issues and changes within the community?	You might speak about any proactive actions you have taken to stay aware of the social issues in your community, such as listening to national and local news regularly and subscribing to newsletters from local authorities and community organisations.

Questions Concerning "Maturity and Sound Temperament"

Magistrates must be able to relate to and work with others, have a sense of fairness, be considerate and courteous, and be open-minded and willing to consider the views and advice of others.

Questions	Suggested Responses
Why do you believe you possess the maturity and sound temperament required to be a magistrate? Provide examples from your experience.	Summarise your relevant experiences, emphasising situations where your maturity and sound temperament were evident. You can mention any leadership roles you have taken on or experiences that required you to handle complex and sensitive matters. Discuss your commitment to fairness, your ability to remain composed, and your collaborative nature.
Can you describe a time when you had to work collaboratively with others to achieve a common goal?	Highlight your ability to relate to and work effectively with different individuals and teams. You can discuss your experiences in group projects or work environments where you had to consider diverse perspectives and reach a consensus. It is important to mention your ability to listen actively, communicate respectfully, and contribute constructively to achieve shared objectives.
How do you ensure fairness and impartiality in your decision-making?	Emphasise your commitment to fairness and the principles of justice. You can discuss your ability to separate personal biases from professional judgements and your track record of making impartial decisions. Your approach and ability to consider all relevant factors, seek diverse opinions and guidance, and apply the law objectively to ensure fairness can be highlighted.
How do you stay open-minded and receptive to different viewpoints and advice?	Discuss your approach to seeking diverse perspectives and valuing the input of others. You should mention your willingness to listen attentively, ask probing questions, and consider alternative viewpoints before reaching conclusions. You can provide examples of situations where you changed your opinions or adjusted your course of action based on new information or feedback. You should also highlight your ability

	to engage in constructive debates and contribute to a collaborative decision-making process.
How would you handle a situation where a defendant became angry or disruptive during a hearing?	This question is designed to test your ability to remain calm and professional in difficult situations. The panel wants to know if you have the necessary skills to manage challenging behaviour in the courtroom.

Questions About "Sound Judgement"

Magistrates must be able to think logically, weigh arguments and reach a balanced decision, be objective, and have the ability to recognise and set aside their prejudices.

Questions	Suggested Responses
Can you provide an example of a situation where you had to think logically, weigh arguments, and reach a balanced decision? How did you approach it, and what was the outcome?	Provide a specific example demonstrating your ability to analyse information, consider multiple perspectives, and make a fair decision. For instance, you could talk about a situation where you had to mediate a dispute between two parties or a complex decision you made in your professional career that required careful consideration.
As a magistrate, you will be expected to be objective and set aside personal prejudices. How do you ensure your personal beliefs and biases do not influence your decision-making process?	Emphasise your commitment to impartiality and provide strategies you use to ensure you remain objective. You could mention actively listening to all sides of an argument, considering the evidence presented, being aware of your own biases, and consciously setting them aside.
Magistrates often encounter situations where they need to make quick decisions under pressure. How do you maintain your ability to think logically and weigh arguments effectively in such situations?	Highlight your ability to remain composed and think critically even under pressure. You could mention your commitment to staying updated with legal knowledge, relying on established guidelines and precedents and remaining focused on the facts and evidence to make informed decisions swiftly.
How do you feel about the possibility of sentencing someone to prison?	Acknowledge the serious nature of sentencing someone to prison but explain that your role as a magistrate would be to uphold the law and ensure that justice is served. If the evidence and circumstances indicate that a prison sentence is appropriate and necessary to maintain public safety, deter future criminal behaviour or provide a just

	resolution, you would not hesitate to make that decision within the bounds of the law.
What would you do if unsure about a legal point or procedure?	The interview panel wants to know how you would handle situations where you are uncertain about the law or procedure. A possible response could be that you would seek guidance from the legal advisor in the court.

Questions Regarding "Commitment and Reliability"

Magistrates must be willing and able to undertake at least 13 sitting days, or (where that is not possible) 26 half-day sittings per year and mandatory training; be able to undertake their duties regularly.

Questions	Suggested Responses
As a magistrate, you are required to undertake a minimum number of sitting days and mandatory training. How do you plan to ensure that you meet these obligations consistently?	Emphasise your understanding of the time requirements and your willingness to meet them consistently. Mention your employer's support for taking time off for public duties if applicable.
Can you provide examples of situations where you have demonstrated commitment and reliability?	Mention instances from your personal or professional lives where you have shown dedication, perseverance, and dependability. You can discuss your involvement in long-term projects, voluntary work, or situations where you consistently met deadlines and fulfilled your responsibilities. It is important to highlight your ability to follow through on commitments, be punctual, and maintain high reliability.
How do you approach working with others?	Highlight your strong communication skills, ability to work well with others, and building positive relationships with people from all backgrounds. You can provide examples of situations where you worked well as part of a team, demonstrated active listening skills, and treated others with respect and courtesy. It is important for you to highlight your open-mindedness and willingness to consider different perspectives, as this is crucial for impartial decision-making. You should emphasise your ability to promote

	fairness and create an inclusive and supportive environment.
What motivates you to commit to the time and effort required to be a magistrate, and how will you sustain this commitment over time?	Share your motivations, such as a sense of duty, giving back to the community, or personal values. Describe your plan for maintaining your commitment, including strategies for staying motivated, seeking support, and managing long-term engagement in the role.
In what ways do you believe you can contribute to maintaining the reputation and integrity of the judiciary system as a magistrate?	Share your understanding of the importance of maintaining the reputation and integrity of the judiciary system. Discuss your personal values and commitment to upholding justice, fairness, and the rule of law. Talk about your dedication to continuous learning, staying updated with legal developments, and acting as a role model for others. Highlight any relevant experience or skills that can contribute positively to the judiciary system.

Scenario-Based Questions

Scenario / Questions	Suggested Responses
A defendant pleads guilty to a minor theft charge. They have no previous convictions. How would you approach sentencing?	You consider the defendant's lack of previous convictions, the nature and value of the theft, and any mitigating factors such as remorse or personal circumstances. A possible sentence could include a conditional discharge, a fine, or a community order, depending on the case details.
During a trial, a witness becomes very emotional and struggles to give evidence. How do you handle this situation?	You would ensure the witness feels supported, possibly taking a short recess to allow them to compose themselves. You would remind them of the importance of their testimony and ensure they understand the process, providing reassurance without influencing their evidence.
You are faced with conflicting oral evidence from witnesses in a domestic abuse case. How do you assess the credibility of their statements?	You evaluate the consistency of their statements, their demeanour, and any supporting evidence. You consider the context and any possible biases or motivations. You also pay attention to the details that corroborate other evidence presented in the case.

A defendant fails to appear in court for their trial. What actions would you take?	You would consider the reasons for the absence, such as a legitimate excuse or notification of illness. Depending on the circumstances, you might decide to adjourn the case or proceed in their absence if the other parties are ready.
A defendant has a history of reoffending and is back in court for a similar offence. How do you approach this case?	You review the defendant's criminal record, the circumstances of the current offence, and any patterns of behaviour. Considering the need for both rehabilitation and public protection, you might impose a stricter sentence, such as a community order with specific requirements or a custodial sentence, if deemed appropriate.
A defendant expresses their belief that they are being unfairly targeted due to their ethnicity. How would you address their concerns while maintaining judicial impartiality?	You would listen carefully to the defendant's concerns, ensure they feel heard, and review the case details to ensure no bias. You would emphasise the court's commitment to fairness and equality.
A defendant appears in court who speaks very little English. How would you ensure that they understand the proceedings and can participate effectively?	You should ensure an interpreter is present to translate all proceedings for the defendant. Additionally, confirm that the defendant understands the charges, their rights, and any court procedures. It is important to be patient and provide clear, concise instructions.
A police officer was injured while apprehending a suspect. The Crown prosecutor is seeking a compensation order. How would you approach this case?	You would carefully consider the evidence presented, including the severity of the injury, the circumstances under which the injury occurred, and any contributory negligence. You would also review the relevant guidelines and precedents to determine if a compensation order is warranted and the appropriate amount.
Someone in the public gallery is causing a disturbance during a trial. How do you handle the situation as a presiding justice?	In this scenario, you might direct the court usher to address the situation by requesting the individual to maintain silence or leave the courtroom if required. It is of utmost importance to maintain order and respect for the judicial process by ensuring that the trial proceeds without any interruptions.
You disagree with your fellow magistrates on the appropriate sentence for a defendant. How do you resolve this disagreement?	You would discuss the reasons for your differing opinions, considering the sentencing guidelines and the case facts. Through respectful deliberation and weighing all viewpoints, you aim to

	reach a consensus that reflects the principles of justice.

USEFUL RESOURCES FOR ASPIRING MAGISTRATES

If you are interested in becoming a magistrate in the UK, there are several resources you can refer to for detailed information and guidance. Here are some useful links:

GOV.UK - Become a Magistrate: This official government page provides comprehensive information on the role of a magistrate, the application process, and the qualifications required. https://www.gov.uk/become-magistrate

Magistrates Association: This charity supports magistrates in England and Wales. Their website offers insights into the role, the benefits, and the application process. https://www.magistrates-association.org.uk/

Judiciary of England and Wales - Magistrates: This official site provides information on the judiciary, including the role and responsibilities of magistrates, application procedures, and training requirements.
https://www.judiciary.uk/

Sentencing Council for England and Wales: The Sentencing Council provides guidelines on sentencing for magistrates and judges. It's an essential resource for understanding how sentences are determined.
https://www.sentencingcouncil.org.uk/

His Majesty's Courts and Tribunals Service (HMCTS): Provides operational support and guidance for courts and tribunals, including magistrates' courts. https://www.gov.uk/government/organisations/hm-courts-and-tribunals-service

The Law Society of England and Wales: Although primarily for solicitors, it offers resources and news that can be useful for understanding the legal environment in which magistrates operate. https://www.lawsociety.org.uk/

Summary of Chapter 13
The Justice System

- **Introduction to Magistracy**: Bukky was introduced to the idea of becoming a magistrate while working on the Operation Black Vote campaign in 1998. This led her to pursue a role in the judiciary, ultimately becoming a Justice of the Peace in 2002 after a rigorous application process.
- **Role and Responsibilities of Magistrates**: Magistrates, also known as Justices of the Peace, handle many cases, including minor criminal offences, family matters, and civil disputes. They offer their time and do not need formal legal qualifications but receive specialised training.
- **Contribution to the Justice System**: Magistrates play an essential role in alleviating the burden on higher courts by making decisions on minor offences and conducting preliminary hearings. They bring local knowledge and fairness to the justice system.
- **Becoming a Magistrate**: The process to become a magistrate includes meeting eligibility criteria, completing court visits, submitting an application, and going through assessments, interviews, and background checks. Successful candidates receive comprehensive training from the Judicial College.
- **Ongoing Support and Mentorship**: Magistrates undergo continuous professional development, with new magistrates receiving mentorship for the first 12-18 months. This ensures they remain effective in their role and fairly uphold the principles of justice.

CHAPTER 14

THE EDUCATION SECTOR

When my children were young, I first became involved in school governance at their primary school. Like many parents, I wanted to play an active role in their education. But being a school governor turned out to be much more than attending meetings, it was about making decisions that directly impacted the learning environment for all children.

Years later, I found myself in a very different role, serving as the Local Authority cabinet member for education and social care. The responsibilities were greater, and the scope was much larger, but the core of the work remained the same: ensuring every child, regardless of background or ability, had the opportunity to succeed. My journey from school governor to shaping education policy at the council level taught me that leadership often begins in the smallest spaces. What started as a desire to support my children's school grew into a lifelong commitment to improving education and social care for countless others.

The UK's education system relies on dedicated individuals who generously volunteer to serve on school governing bodies to ensure schools are run effectively, transparently, and in the best interests of pupils and students.

Being a school governor requires dedication, a willingness to tackle complex issues, and a commitment to improving education. Their efforts help create schools where students can thrive, teachers perform their best, and communities feel confident in the education system. By driving continuous improvement, governors play a vital part in shaping the next generation of well-educated and responsible citizens.

Functions of School Governors

Although demanding, the role of a school governor is highly rewarding. It offers valuable opportunities for personal and professional growth, equipping governors with leadership, strategic planning, and financial management skills that benefit their careers and daily lives. Beyond skill development, serving as a governor brings a deep sense of fulfillment, knowing that their contributions positively impact schools and the wider community. The following are some of the key responsibilities undertaken by school governors:

Strategic Planning

Setting the school's strategic direction is one of the primary functions of school governors. This involves working with the headteacher and senior leadership team to develop and implement a vision and ethos for the school. School governors help to establish clear objectives and ensure that the school's policies and practices align with its mission and goals. They also play a key role in monitoring and evaluating the school's performance, using data and evidence to hold the headteacher accountable for achieving educational outcomes.

Overseeing Finances

Financial oversight is an important function of school governors. They are responsible for ensuring that the school's budget is managed effectively and that resources are allocated in a way that supports educational objectives. This includes reviewing financial data, approving budgets, and deciding on staffing and allocation of resources. The governing body's effective financial management ensures that the school can continue to operate and offer its students a high-quality education.

Recruiting and Managing Staff

Governors are involved in recruiting senior staff members, particularly the headteacher, and may participate in the selection process for other senior positions. They may also play a role in addressing performance concerns or disciplinary matters, ensuring proper procedures are followed.

Accountability and Safeguarding

School governors must also ensure that the school complies with legal and regulatory requirements. This includes safeguarding children, enhancing their welfare, and ensuring the school follows equality and diversity policies. Governors must be familiar with relevant legislation and ensure the school implements robust policies and procedures to protect students and staff.

Community Engagement

Working with the community is another essential function that school governors play in adding value to the educational establishments they govern. They may serve as a link between the school and its wider community, helping to promote a sense of ownership and involvement among parents, local businesses, and other stakeholders. This engagement can take many forms, from organising events and consultations to participating in local education forums. By developing good relationships with the community, governors may contribute to making the school a welcoming and supportive place for all children.

Key Attributes of Effective School Governors

School governors need to possess a range of qualities and skills to effectively fulfil their roles of providing strategic guidance and support to the school's leadership and staff. These include commitment, communication skills, analytical skills, problem-solving skills, leadership skills, knowledge of education, strategic thinking, ethical behaviour, and a commitment to diversity and inclusion.

1. Commitment:

School governors must be dedicated to their role and willing to invest time and effort into the school's success. Regular attendance at meetings and active participation in the school's decision-making processes are key expectations.

2. Good Communication Skills:

Effective communication is essential. Governors should be able to engage clearly with other governors, school staff, parents, and students. This includes active listening, clear verbal communication, and concise written skills.

3. Analytical Skills:

Governors must be able to interpret and analyse data, including financial reports, performance indicators, and other key information. These analytical skills are crucial for making informed decisions.

4. Problem-Solving Skills:

Effective school governors need to identify problems and develop practical solutions. A proactive approach to tackling issues is essential in maintaining a positive school environment.

5. Leadership Skills:

Governors should possess strong leadership capabilities and be able to inspire and collaborate with fellow governors and school staff. They must be able to set clear goals and help develop strategies to achieve them.

6. Knowledge of Education:

An understanding of the education sector is fundamental. Governors should be familiar with curriculum requirements, assessment processes, and policies that impact the school's functioning.

7. Strategic Thinking:

Governors should think strategically, planning for the school's long-term goals. They must be able to identify future priorities and create actionable plans to achieve them.

8. Ethical Behaviour:

Governors must display integrity and ethical behaviour in all aspects of their work. Transparency and accountability are crucial, ensuring that decisions and actions align with the school's values.

9. Time Management:

Effective time management is key for governors, as their role often requires attending meetings, reading reports, and regularly visiting the school. Prioritising responsibilities and staying organised is essential.

10. Commitment to Diversity and Inclusion:

School governors should be committed to promoting diversity and inclusion within the school. They need to be mindful of the needs of all students and work to ensure that the school remains a welcoming and inclusive environment for everyone.

Types of School Governors:

School governors form part of a governing body that brings together parents, staff, local authority representatives, and community members. This diverse mix ensures a broad range of perspectives and expertise, contributing to well-rounded decision-making in school management. In the UK, there are different types of school governors, each with similar roles and responsibilities. Their titles reflect their specific category and the process through which they are appointed.

1. **Parent Governors**: These governors are elected by parents of children attending the school. They bring a parental viewpoint to discussions and decision-making processes within the governing body. Parent governors

are valuable in ensuring that the school's policies and practices resonate with the needs and expectations of parents and families.

2. **Staff Governors**: Typically elected by the school staff, including teachers and support staff. They bring the perspective of the school's workforce to the governing body and contribute to discussions on matters affecting staff and pupils.
3. **Local Authority Governors**: These governors are appointed by the local authority that maintains the school. They serve as a link between the local authority and the school, ensuring that local policies and priorities are reflected in the school's governance.
4. **Co-opted Governors**: Chosen by the governing body based on their skills, experience, community links, or connections that are deemed beneficial to the school. Co-opted governors are not necessarily directly affiliated with the school but are chosen for their potential to contribute effectively to the governing body's functions. Co-opted governors often bring specialised knowledge in areas such as finance, law, or strategic planning.
5. **Foundation Governors**: Found in schools with a religious or foundation trust background, these governors are appointed by the school's founding body or trust. They ensure that the school operates in accordance with its founding principles, ethos, and religious values while also fulfilling the broader educational objectives set by the governing body.
6. **Sponsor Governors**: Found in academies and free schools, sponsor governors are appointed by the school's sponsor or academy trust. They bring education and business management expertise to support the school's improvement and development.

Becoming a School Governor

In the UK, becoming a school governor typically involves expressing interest to the school or local authority when vacancies arise. Depending on the type of governorship, the process may involve nomination, election, or appointment based on specific criteria such as skills, experience, and community involvement.

Generally, individuals interested in becoming governors should have a genuine interest in education, a commitment to improving student outcomes, and the willingness to devote time and effort to the role. Here are the typical steps to becoming a school governor:

- **Identify Vacancies**: Schools often advertise governor vacancies through their websites, newsletters, or local authority channels. Prospective governors can also inquire directly with the school or governing body about upcoming openings.
- **Submit an Application**: Depending on the type of governorship (e.g., parent, staff, co-opted), interested individuals may need to submit an application or nomination form. This may involve outlining their background, skills, and reasons for wanting to become a governor.
- **Selection Process**: The selection process varies but often includes reviewing applications, interviews, or discussions with current governors or school leadership. This ensures that the candidates' skills and experiences align with the needs of the governing body.
- **Appointment or Election**: Once selected, governors are appointed (in the case of co-opted or appointed governors) or elected (in the case of parent or staff governors) to the governing body for a term of four years.
- **DBS (Disclosure and Barring Service):** Prospective governors are often required to undergo checks such as a Disclosure and Barring Service (DBS) check to ensure they are suitable to work with children and young people.
- **Induction and Training**: Training and support are usually provided to new governors to familiarise them with the school, its policies, and their roles and responsibilities. This includes understanding educational policies, financial management, and the legal framework within which schools operate. Ongoing training and development opportunities are

also available to ensure governors remain effective. Many governors find the role rewarding as they contribute directly to improving educational outcomes and shaping the future of young people in their communities. You could consider becoming a school governor as a way to give back to your community and serve others.

Useful Resources and Links for Potential School Governors

If you are considering becoming a school governor or if you are already serving in that capacity, many organisations and services offer valuable advice and support. These links provide valuable information on understanding the role, offering practical guidance, and exploring opportunities for ongoing professional development.

GOV.UK – Become a School Governor: This official government page offers a comprehensive overview of the role of a school governor, including responsibilities, eligibility, and how to apply. It also provides links to further resources and guidance documents. https://www.gov.uk/become-school-college-governor

Inspiring Governance: This platform connects skilled volunteers with schools needing governors. It offers resources on the roles and responsibilities of school governors, training opportunities, and support in matching with a suitable school. https://www.inspiringgovernance.org

Governors for Schools: This organisation recruits and places volunteers as governors in schools across England. They offer resources on the responsibilities of governors, training modules, and support networks for existing governors. https://governorsforschools.org.uk

Governors for Schools: This charity connects skilled volunteers with schools in need of governors. They provide information on becoming a governor, training resources, and support for new and existing governors. https://governorsforschools.org.uk

Get Information about Schools (GIAS): This website offers a searchable database of all schools in England. This resource is useful for finding specific information about schools, including governance details and performance data. https://get-information-schools.service.gov.uk/

National Governance Association (NGA): The NGA is a key organisation that provides a wealth of resources to school governors. This includes guidance on best practices, training opportunities, policy templates, and updates on educational legislation and governance news. https://www.nga.org.uk

The Key for School Governors: This subscription-based service provides practical resources and guidance tailored specifically for school governors. It includes articles, policy templates, case studies, and a Q&A service with experts in school governance. https://thekeysupport.com

Modern Governor: Modern Governor provides online training modules for school governors. These modules cover various topics, including governance basics, safeguarding, financial oversight, and strategic planning. https://www.moderngovernor.com

GovernorHub: GovernorHub is an online platform that helps governing boards manage their work. It includes features for document storage, communication, meeting management, and access to resources and updates on governance issues. https://governorhub.com

Ofsted: Ofsted is the Office for Standards in Education, Children's Services and Skills. It provides inspection reports and regulatory guidelines crucial for governors to understand the performance and compliance of their schools. https://www.gov.uk/government/organisations/ofsted

Local Authorities and Councils: Local councils often provide specific guidance and support for school governors within their jurisdiction. This can include training opportunities, local governance policies, and forums for networking and sharing best practices. Check your local council's website.

SUMMARY OF CHAPTER 14
THE EDUCATION SECTOR

- **Journey from School Governor to Policy Leadership** – The chapter highlights the author's transition from a school governor to a Local Authority cabinet member for education and social care, emphasising how grassroots school involvement can lead to broader influence in shaping education policies.
- **Role and Responsibilities of School Governors** – School governors play a vital role in setting strategic direction, overseeing finances, recruiting senior staff, ensuring accountability, and engaging with the community to improve education outcomes.
- **Key Skills and Attributes of Effective Governors** – Governors require commitment, strong communication, analytical thinking, leadership, problem-solving abilities, and an understanding of education policies to support school management and improvement effectively.
- **Types of School Governors and Their Contributions** – Different categories of school governors, such as parent, staff, local authority, co-opted, foundation, and sponsor governors, bring diverse perspectives and expertise to school governance.
- **Pathway to Becoming a School Governor** – The chapter outlines the process of becoming a governor, including identifying vacancies, applying, undergoing selection and DBS checks, and participating in training while also providing useful resources for prospective governors.

CHAPTER 15

THE HEALTH SECTOR

The United Kingdom's National Health Service (NHS) is well-known worldwide for delivering comprehensive public healthcare services.

While frontline healthcare professionals such as doctors, nurses, and paramedics play critical roles in providing direct patient care, there are countless other opportunities and platforms for individuals to serve the public and contribute to the healthcare system.

The Royal London Hospital NHS

Opportunities to serve include being an NHS Foundation Trust member, an NHS Foundation Trust Governor, an NHS non-executive director, serving on Fitness to Practice Panels, and participating in other governance and quality control roles. Each of these responsibilities contributes to the NHS's overall effectiveness and efficiency. The contribution ensures that the NHS remains responsible, efficient, and continuously improving. They are rewarding approaches to having a big impact on healthcare delivery. Here we look at some of these opportunities, highlighting how individuals can become involved and make a difference.

The National Health Service (NHS) Foundation Trust

NHS Foundation Trusts function as partially independent organisations within the NHS England. Established to deliver healthcare services, they operate with a degree of independence from the Department of Health, enabling them to deliver services that best meet the specific needs of their local communities. Each Foundation Trust is run by a board of directors and is accountable to its members, which include patients, staff, and the public. They focus on improving efficiency, quality of care, and patient experience, often through innovative practices and financial flexibility. These trusts aim to provide high standards of healthcare tailored to community needs. Individuals can become members of one of these trusts and gain a say in the management of their local health services.

The Role and Impact of Members

The purpose of joining an NHS Trust is to promote a stronger connection between the trust and the community it serves. This helps ensure that the services offered align with the needs and preferences of patients and the public. Individuals can contribute to the promotion of a culture of continuous improvement and high standards in healthcare delivery. Members elect governors, shape decisions regarding services and priorities, and make valuable contributions to the trust's strategic direction. Through active participation in meetings and consultations, members play a crucial role in upholding the trust's accountability to the public it serves. The roles and activities can vary slightly between NHS Foundation Trusts but generally cover the following areas:

Role	Activities	Public Benefits
Governance	• Electing the Council of Governors. • Holding the Board of Directors to account.	• Ensures transparency and accountability in the Trust's operations. • Promotes high standards of care and management.
Community Representation	• Providing a voice for the local community and staff. • Participating in members' meetings and forums.	• Reflects the diverse needs and priorities of the community. • Enhances trust and responsiveness to community concerns.
Strategic Input	• Contributing to the development of Trust strategies and policies. • Offering feedback on service plans and major decisions.	• Ensures that services are aligned with public needs. • Helps in shaping policies that improve patient care and services
Support and Promotion	• Advocating for the Trust in the Community. • Participating in public engagement and information campaigns.	• Increases public awareness and understanding of Trust services. • Builds stronger community relationships and support.
Recruitment and Selection	• Involvement in the appointment of key personnel, such as Non-Executive Directors. • Participating in interview panels and selection processes.	• Ensures that leadership roles are filled by competent and community-minded individuals. • Enhances leadership quality.
Feedback and Improvement	• Gathering and relaying feedback from patients, staff, and the public. • Participating in focus groups and consultations.	• Helps identify areas for improvement in patient care and services.

Role	Activities	Public Benefits
		• Encourages a culture of continuous improvement.
Education and Training	• Participating in training sessions and workshops to gain a deeper understanding of their roles and responsibilities. • Engaging in continuous learning about healthcare issues.	• Enhances the effectiveness and informed decision-making of members. • Promotes informed and skilled community input.
Monitoring Performance	• Reviewing performance reports and financial statements. • Engaging in quality and safety reviews and inspections	• Ensures the Trust meets its performance targets and financial obligations. • Promotes high standards of care and safety.
Consultation and Decision Making	• Participating in formal consultations on significant changes or proposals. • Voting on key issues affecting the Trust's direction and operations.	• Ensures major decisions are made with broad community input. • Enhances the democratic governance of the Trust.
Innovative Ideas and Research	• Bringing forward innovative ideas and suggestions for service improvement. • Supporting research initiatives and new projects	• Drives innovation in service delivery and patient care. • Supports the adoption of best practices and new technologies.

How to Join Your NHS Foundation Trust

Joining an NHS Foundation Trust is generally simple. If you are over 16 years old, live in the area served by the trust, or have been a patient or service user, you can apply for membership. Most NHS Trusts provide a membership section on their website where you can sign up online. Alternatively, you can complete a membership form available at trust facilities. Once your application is processed, the trust will confirm your membership by sending you a welcome pack or a confirmation email.

NHS Foundation Trust Governors

While general members of an NHS Foundation Trust can vote in elections and participate in consultations, the role of a Governor within an NHS Foundation Trust is much more involved. Governors are elected or appointed to represent the interests of the trust's members and the wider community, providing oversight and holding the trust's Board of Directors accountable for the performance and strategic direction of the trust. This elevated responsibility allows Governors to significantly influence the trust's governance and ensure that it remains patient-focused and financially sustainable.

The Role and Impact of Governors

The role of NHS Foundation Trust Governors is vital in ensuring the Trust operates with transparency, effectiveness, and in the public's best interests. They are responsible for governance, accountability, strategic oversight, and engagement, all of which contribute to the overall quality and responsiveness of healthcare services.

Role	Activities	Public Benefits
Holding the Board to Account	• Attending and participating in Council of Governors meetings. • Asking questions and seeking assurance from the Board of Directors. • Reviewing performance reports and financial statements.	• Ensures transparency and accountability of the Trust's operations. • Enhances the quality of care and services provided.
Representing the Interests of Members and the Public	• Engaging with members and the wider public to gather feedback and concerns.	• Reflects public and patient views in decision-making.

Role	Activities	Public Benefits
	• Participating in public forums and events. • Communicating effectively with stakeholders.	• Builds trust and ensures services meet the community's needs.
Appointing and Removing the Chair and Non-Executive Directors	• Participating in the recruitment and selection process. • Conducting performance reviews and appraisals. • Making decisions on reappointments or removals.	• Ensures strong and effective leadership. • Maintains high standards of governance and accountability.
Approving Significant Transactions	• Reviewing and analysing proposals for major transactions. • Assessing the potential impact on services and finances. • Voting on whether to approve or reject significant deals.	• Protects the Trust's financial stability and sustainability. • Ensures that major decisions benefit patients and the community.
Strategic Planning and Development	• Contributing to the development of the Trust's strategic direction. • Reviewing and influencing long-term plans and objectives. • Ensuring plans align with public interest and needs.	• Ensures the Trust evolves to meet future healthcare demands. • Supports the delivery of high-quality, patient-centred care.
Monitoring Quality of Care	• Reviewing patient care reports and clinical performance data. • Engaging with patient groups and visiting care facilities. • Working with Quality and Safety Committees.	• Promotes continuous improvement in care standards. • Ensures patient safety and positive health outcomes.
Financial Oversight	• Analysing financial statements and budgets.	• Ensures efficient use of resources and public funds.

Role	Activities	Public Benefits
	• Monitoring financial performance against targets. • Addressing financial risks and challenges.	• Maintains the financial health of the Trust to support ongoing services.
Engaging in Stakeholder Communication	• Facilitating communication between the Trust and its members. • Providing regular updates and reports. • Hosting and participating in stakeholder meetings.	• Keeps the public informed and engaged with Trust activities. • Fosters a culture of openness and collaboration.

How to Become an NHS Foundation Trust Governor

Becoming a Governor of an NHS Foundation Trust usually involves nomination and election by the trust's members. These elections occur regularly, giving members the chance to run for office. Successful candidates typically demonstrate a strong commitment to public service and a solid understanding of the healthcare sector.

To be eligible for election, one must generally be a member of the NHS Foundation Trust. Membership is open to anyone over 16 who lives in the area served by the trust or has been a patient or carer within the trust's services, though some trusts may have additional criteria.

Most Governors are elected by the trust's members. Prospective candidates must submit a nomination form outlining their interests and qualifications. Campaigning may involve sharing their vision and objectives with the electorate, often through written statements or hustings events.

In addition to elected positions, some Governors are appointed to represent specific stakeholder groups such as local authorities, universities, or staff members. These appointments are typically made by the relevant organisations or bodies.

Once elected or appointed, Governors usually undergo an induction process to understand their roles and responsibilities. They also have access to ongoing training and development opportunities to help them perform their duties effectively.

Non-Executive NHS Trust Board Directors

An organisation's governance, especially in public sectors like the National Health Service (NHS), relies heavily on the contributions of executive and non-executive directors. They play distinct yet complementary roles. Executive Directors are full-time employees responsible for the day-to-day operations and implementing the board's decisions. In contrast, Non-Executive Directors (NEDs) provide independent oversight, bring external perspectives, and ensure accountability, acting as a critical check on the executives.

The public's involvement is crucial in these roles, particularly for NEDs, as they often come from varied professional backgrounds, contributing diverse skills and insights. This enhances the board's decision-making process and ensures that the NHS remains aligned with community needs and values. NEDs' voluntary service embodies civic responsibility and commitment to public welfare, making them invaluable assets to the NHS. Their act of service deserves commendation as they safeguard the integrity and effectiveness of the NHS, ensuring it remains a pillar of the UK's healthcare system. Public engagement helps maintain transparency and trust in these vital roles.

Role and Functions of NEDs on NHS Trust Boards

The role of NEDs is crucial in upholding the public's trust and confidence in the NHS. When community members actively participate, their valuable perspectives and expertise can greatly improve the quality and efficiency of the healthcare system. Serving as a non-executive director in the public sector is not just a way to give back to society but also a highly rewarding pursuit that profoundly impacts the lives of countless individuals. Their responsibilities typically include the following:

- **Strategic Guidance**: Non-executive directors contribute to shaping the strategic direction of the NHS Trust. They help ensure that the organisation's goals align with its mission to provide high-quality healthcare services.
- **Oversight and Governance**: NEDs oversee the implementation of policies and procedures, ensuring that the trust operates within regulatory frameworks and follows best governance practices.
- **Risk Management**: They play a key role in identifying, assessing, and mitigating risks. By offering an external perspective, they help safeguard the trust against potential pitfalls.
- **Ethics and Integrity**: Upholding the highest standards of ethics and integrity is a fundamental duty of non-executive directors. They ensure that the Trust operates consistently with public sector values and the ethical standards expected of a healthcare provider.
- **Performance Evaluation**: Non-executive directors participate in evaluating the executive team's performance. They ensure that executives are held accountable for their actions and that the trust's performance metrics are met.
- **Financial Oversight**: They scrutinise financial reports, budgets, and audits to ensure fiscal responsibility and the effective use of public funds.
- **Stakeholder Engagement**: NEDs engage with various stakeholders, including patients, staff, and the broader community, ensuring that the trust's services meet public expectations and needs.

Characteristics of Effective Non-Executive Directors

To fulfil the role and functions effectively, non-executive directors on NHS Trust boards need to possess certain characteristics:

- **Independence**: The role of NEDs requires them to maintain independence from the management team to offer unbiased judgement and effectively challenge the status quo without any conflicts of interest.

- **Leadership and Strategic Thinking**: The ability to contribute to long-term planning and decision-making.
- **Experience and Expertise**: They should bring a wealth of experience from various sectors, including healthcare, finance, governance, and public policy, to provide a well-rounded perspective.
- **Analytical Skills**: Strong analytical skills are essential for assessing complex information and making informed decisions.
- **Communication Skills**: Effective communication skills are crucial for engaging with stakeholders, articulating strategic visions, and influencing board discussions.
- **Commitment**: NEDs should be committed to dedicating adequate time and effort to fulfil their duties diligently, often participating in multiple board meetings, committees, and stakeholder engagements.
- **Integrity and Accountability**: A commitment to ethical practices and transparency.

How to Join the NHS Trust Board as a Non-Executive Director

To become an NED, a strong background in leadership, finance, clinical services, or governance is typically required. Job vacancies can be found on the NHS Jobs website, NHS improvement website, public appointments website, and other professional platforms. Additionally, you can connect with organisations specialising in board-level recruitment. The application process requires the submission of an application and CV, which are then followed by interviews. Successful candidates often undergo training to familiarise themselves with the NHS's specific challenges and regulations.

Summary of Chapter 15
The Health Sector

- **Opportunities in NHS Governance**: Individuals can contribute to the healthcare system by serving as NHS Foundation Trust members, Governors, Non-Executive Directors, or participating in Fitness to Practice Panels. These roles enhance NHS accountability, efficiency, and quality of care.
- **NHS Foundation Trusts and Public Engagement**: NHS Foundation Trusts operate with some independence, allowing them to tailor services to local needs. Members help shape decisions, elect Governors, and provide strategic input to ensure continuous improvement in patient care.
- **Role of NHS Governors**: Elected or appointed NHS Foundation Trust Governors hold Boards accountable, represent community interests, influence strategic planning, and participate in leadership selection to maintain high healthcare standards.
- **Non-Executive Directors in NHS Trusts**: NEDs provide independent oversight, ensure ethical governance, manage risks, and oversee financial performance. Their external expertise enhances decision-making and upholds public trust in NHS services.
- **Pathways to Participation**: Joining an NHS Foundation Trust or becoming a Governor or NED involves a nomination and election process, requiring commitment to public service, governance knowledge, and leadership skills. Training and development opportunities are available for those taking on these roles.

PART FIVE

CHAMPIONS OF ACCOUNTABILITY

Chapter 16

Fitness to Practice Panels

One day, a friend who served as a lay member on a Fitness to Practice (FtP) panel shared her experience with me. She told me about the difficult decisions they had to make, for example, balancing patient safety with giving professionals a fair opportunity to explain their actions. It wasn't just about enforcing rules; it was about ensuring that the public could continue to trust those in the medical profession.

Her story interested me, and I started learning more about the role of FtP panels in maintaining ethical standards in healthcare. These panels were not just about discipline; they provided opportunities for rehabilitation and retraining and allowed professionals to correct their mistakes where possible.

It became clear to me that serving on a Fitness to Practice panel is a powerful act of service. It allows people from different backgrounds to ensure that those entrusted with people's health and well-being meet the highest standards. It's not always easy, but it's an essential role that helps keep public confidence in vital institutions strong.

These FtP panels, which include both professionals and lay members, are essential to the regulatory framework for professionals such as those in health and social care, ensuring practitioners adhere to required standards and remain competent. Bodies such as the General Medical Council (GMC), Nursing and Midwifery Council (NMC), and Health and Care Professions Council (HCPC) all use these panels in their operational frameworks. They review cases where a healthcare professional's conduct, competence, or health may impair their ability to practice safely and effectively.

Through their service, individual lay members contribute to upholding high standards in healthcare, thereby protecting patient safety and maintaining public trust in the profession. Serving on an FtP panel is a substantial responsibility that demands fairness, integrity, and impartiality. It requires rigorous training and a thorough understanding of the ethical and legal frameworks governing healthcare practice.

Role and Function of Fitness to Practice Panels

Lay members bring an invaluable perspective to these panels. Their role ensures that the public's voice is represented in decision-making, promoting transparency and accountability. They help assess whether a healthcare professional's fitness to practice is compromised and determine appropriate actions, ranging from additional training and supervision to suspension or removal from the professional register. The primary functions of FtP panels include:

- **Assessing Complaints and Allegations**: FtP panels review complaints or allegations made against healthcare professionals. This can include issues related to misconduct, incompetence, or breaches of professional guidelines.
- **Conducting Hearings**: When a case is referred to a hearing, the FtP panel conducts a formal process to analyse the evidence, hear testimonies from witnesses, and consider the statements from the healthcare professional involved.
- **Making Decisions**: Based on the evidence presented, the FtP panel determines whether the healthcare professional is fit to practice. This can result in various outcomes, including no action, issuing a warning, imposing conditions on practice, suspension, or removal from the professional register.

- **Ensuring Public Safety**: The overarching aim of FtP panels is to safeguard the public by ensuring that only those who are competent and adhere to professional standards are allowed to practice.

How to Join Fitness to Practice Panels

The process of joining a Fitness to Practice (FtP) panel involves requirements that may vary slightly depending on the regulatory body. If you're interested in joining, it's crucial to thoroughly review the specific requirements and opportunities with the relevant regulatory bodies, such as the General Medical Council (GMC), the Nursing and Midwifery Council (NMC), or other professional healthcare regulators in the UK.

Generally, potential panel members often need a background in healthcare, law, or other relevant fields, though lay members (those without a professional healthcare background) are also encouraged to apply to ensure diverse perspectives. Interested individuals must apply to the relevant regulatory body, which usually includes a CV and an application explaining their interest and suitability for the role. Successful applicants will then be invited for an interview and may be required to provide references.

New panel members undergo a comprehensive training and induction program covering the regulatory framework, the role and responsibilities of panel members, and how to conduct hearings and make decisions impartially. After completing the training, individuals are formally appointed to the FtP panel for a fixed term, often around three to four years, with the possibility of reappointment. Panel members are also expected to participate in ongoing training and development to stay updated with regulations and best practice changes.

Other Health and Social Care Opportunities

Additional health and social care opportunities are available for individuals to contribute to public welfare. These include participation in Healthwatch, clinical commissioning groups (CCGs), health ambassador roles, and organisations such as the National Institute for Health and Care Excellence (NICE). By getting involved in these opportunities, individuals can contribute to improving health and social care services, ensuring they meet the community's needs and promote public well-being.

Opportunities	Description	How to get involved
Healthwatch	Healthwatch is an independent national champion for people who use health and social care services. It exists in two forms: • **Healthwatch England**: Provides leadership, support, and advice to the local Healthwatch networks. • **Local Healthwatch**: Found in each area, local Healthwatch organisations gather the views of local residents about their experiences with health and social care services. They work to ensure that the voices of patients, service users, and the public are heard and influence decision-making processes at both local and national levels.	Individuals can become Healthwatch volunteers, providing feedback on services, conducting research, and helping to raise awareness. Visit the Healthwatch website and find your local Healthwatch to learn about specific opportunities.
Patient Participation Groups (PPGs)	PPGs are groups of patients working with local GP practices to improve services and promote health and well-being. They provide a platform for patients to give feedback and contribute to the planning and delivery of health services.	Patients can join their local PPG by inquiring at their GP practice. Meetings are typically held regularly, and participants can contribute by attending meetings, sharing their experiences, and working on projects.
Integrated Care System (ICS)	ICSs are partnerships that bring together providers and	Individuals can engage with their local ICS by attending

Opportunities	Description	How to get involved
	commissioners of NHS services with local authorities and other partners to plan and deliver joined-up health and care services.	public meetings, participating in consultations, and joining patient and public involvement forums to share their insights and feedback.
Health Ambassadors	Health Ambassadors are individuals who engage with communities to promote health and well-being, particularly targeting hard-to-reach groups. They help disseminate health information, encourage participation in health programs, and act as a bridge between the community and health services.	Interested individuals can volunteer through local health organisations, charities, or public health initiatives. Training and support are usually provided. Interested individuals can contact local NHS trusts or public health departments to learn about opportunities.
Patient and Public Involvement (PPI) in Research	Patients and the public can participate in health research through PPI groups. This involvement can range from helping to design research studies and ensuring that research is patient-centred, to participating in advisory panels or steering groups.	Individuals can participate by joining research advisory groups, becoming lay advisors on research projects, or participating in clinical trials and studies. Information is typically available through research institutions, universities, and organisations like INVOLVE, which supports PPI in health research.
National Institute for Health and Care Excellence (NICE)	NICE provides national guidance and advice to improve health and social care. It includes professionals and laypeople in developing its recommendations.	Individuals can get involved by joining the NICE Citizens Council, participating in consultations, becoming a committee member, or engaging in public discussions and feedback sessions on draft guidelines. Visit the NICE website to explore current opportunities and application processes.
Volunteer Roles	Many health and social care organisations offer volunteer opportunities. Volunteers can assist in various capacities,	Contact local hospitals or health trusts to inquire about volunteer programs.

Opportunities	Description	How to get involved
	from providing support in hospitals and care homes to helping out with community health initiatives.	Reach out to local care homes or organisations like Age UK for opportunities.
	NHS and Care Volunteer Responders: The NHS Volunteer Responders program, run by the Royal Voluntary Service, recruits volunteers to help with tasks such as delivering food and medicine, transporting patients, and providing check-in and chat services for those who are isolated.	Individuals can sign up through the NHS Volunteer Responders website.
	Royal Voluntary Service: The Royal Voluntary Service offers roles in hospitals, communities, and emergency response situations. Volunteers can help with ward support, befriending services, and organising activities for the elderly.	Check the Royal Voluntary Service website for current opportunities and application processes.
	St John Ambulance: St John Ambulance provides first aid training and services across the UK. Volunteers can get involved in various roles, including event first aiders, youth leaders, and community advocates.	Interested individuals can apply through the St John Ambulance website.
	Age UK: Age UK is a leading charity for older people. Volunteers can help with services such as befriending, advice and information, and community events.	Prospective volunteers can find opportunities and apply on the Age UK website.

Opportunities	Description	How to get involved
Online Platforms and Social Media	Engaging through online platforms and social media allows individuals to participate in surveys, discussions, and consultations. Organisations like NHS Digital and various health charities often use these tools to gather feedback and involve the public in health-related conversations.	Follow organisations and charities on platforms like Facebook, Twitter, and LinkedIn. They often post about volunteer opportunities and ways to get involved.
Public Consultations	Health and social care services frequently run public consultations to seek input on proposed changes, new services, or policy developments. These consultations can be accessed online or through community events and meetings.	Keep an eye on NHS and local government websites for announcements about upcoming consultations.

Useful Resources and Links for Health and Social Care.

If you're looking to make a positive impact in UK Health and Social Care organisations and contribute to the community, here are some useful resources to help you find an opportunity.

NHS and Care Volunteer Responders: The NHS Volunteer Responders programme was established to provide vital support to the NHS and the care sector amidst the challenges posed by the COVID-19 pandemic. Volunteers assist with various tasks, including delivering groceries and medication, transporting patients, and providing support to those who are isolated. Check out the website nhscarevolunteerresponders.org for more information.

Royal Voluntary Service (RVS): The Royal Voluntary Service is a well-known and respected volunteering organisation in the UK. They offer valuable support to elderly individuals by assisting and contributing to the NHS. They accomplish this by volunteering at hospitals and offering community services like delivering meals and providing companionship. Check out their website at https://www.royalvoluntaryservice.org.uk.

Age UK: Age UK is a charity dedicated to enhancing the lives of older individuals by providing them with valuable support and services. Volunteers have various opportunities to participate in activities like befriending, assisting at day centres, and providing support to local Age UK shops. Find out more at https://www.ageuk.org.uk.

The British Red Cross: The British Red Cross helps individuals in crisis situations, both within the United Kingdom and across the globe. Volunteers can assist in a wide range of services, such as emergency response, first aid, and supporting vulnerable individuals. Check out this link to get involved and volunteer with the Red Cross: https://www.redcross.org.uk/get-involved/volunteer.

Marie Curie: Marie Curie offers compassionate care and support to individuals facing terminal illnesses and their loved ones. Volunteers can make a meaningful impact by offering assistance in hospices, providing companionship, contributing to fundraising efforts, and offering support to needy families. Check out this link for more information on volunteering: https://www.mariecurie.org.uk/get-involved/volunteering.

Mind: Mind is a mental health charity that offers valuable support and guidance to individuals facing mental health challenges. Volunteers can contribute in various roles, including providing peer support and assisting with administrative tasks. Check out this link: https://www.mind.org.uk/information-support.

Macmillan Cancer Support: Macmillan Cancer Support offers support and assistance to individuals and families affected by cancer. Volunteers can contribute in various ways, including providing practical and emotional support, assisting with events, and offering administrative help. Check out this link for some great volunteering opportunities: https://volunteering.macmillan.org.uk/opportunities

Carers UK: Carers UK is a charity that assists unpaid carers. Volunteers can help by providing information and advice, making phone calls to carers, and attending local events and campaigns. Visit https://www.carersuk.org/get-involved/ for more information.

The Care Workers' Charity: The Care Workers' Charity provides financial aid and grants to care workers in times of need. Volunteers can help with fundraising, promoting the charity's work, and providing direct support to care workers. Visit their website at https://www.thecareworkerscharity.org.uk/volunteering/

Alzheimer's Society: The Alzheimer's Society works to improve the lives of people affected by dementia. Volunteers can get involved in various roles, including offering companionship, helping with support groups, and contributing to fundraising efforts. Check out their website: https://www.alzheimers.org.uk

Summary of Chapter 16: Fitness to Practice Panels

- **Role and Importance of FtP Panels** – Fitness to Practice panels ensure healthcare professionals meet ethical and competency standards, balancing public safety with fairness for practitioners.
- **Key Responsibilities** – FtP panels assess complaints, conduct hearings, make disciplinary decisions, and maintain public trust in the profession.
- **Lay Members' Contributions** – Non-medical panel members provide a public perspective, ensuring transparency, accountability, and fair decision-making.
- **How to Join an FtP Panel** – Interested individuals must apply through regulatory bodies (GMC, NMC, HCPC), undergo training, and commit to impartiality and ongoing development.
- **Additional Health & Social Care Roles** – Opportunities exist beyond FtP panels, including Healthwatch, Patient Participation Groups, and volunteering with healthcare charities.

Chapter 17
Non-Executive Directors

In corporate history, few cases highlight the importance of strong governance as clearly as the collapse of Carillion, one of the UK's largest construction and facilities management companies. Before its dramatic failure in 2018, Carillion held billions of pounds in government contracts, overseeing major infrastructure projects, including hospitals, schools, and roads. Yet, beneath the surface, financial mismanagement, risky accounting practices, and a lack of effective oversight led the company towards disaster.

Non-executive directors (NEDs) were meant to provide independent scrutiny, ensuring that the company's leadership acted in the best interests of stakeholders. However, reports later revealed that Carillion's NEDs failed to challenge reckless decision-making and overlooked warning signs of financial instability.

The downfall of Carillion serves as a cautionary tale about what happens when governance fails. It underscores why non-executive directors are more than just advisors; they are vital to ensuring transparency, accountability, and ethical leadership in any organisation. Whether in a corporate boardroom, a public institution, or a charity, NEDs must bring critical thinking, independence, and the courage to ask difficult questions.

This chapter explores what it means to be a non-executive director, the responsibilities of the role, and how individuals can step into this position to contribute to strong governance and ethical leadership.

The Impact of NEDs Across Various Sectors in the UK

Non-executive directors (NEDs) are integral to the governance of organisations across the public, private, and charitable sectors in the UK. They provide independent oversight, strategic guidance, and ethical leadership, ensuring that decisions align with legal standards, stakeholder interests, and long-term sustainability. Unlike executive directors, NEDs do not engage in daily operations but instead bring an external perspective to the boardroom, holding leadership accountable and enhancing good governance.

In the public sector, NEDs play a particularly vital role in organisations such as the NHS, where their expertise helps shape policies that directly impact patient care and operational efficiency. In private and charitable sectors, they support financial stability, risk management, and ethical business practices, contributing to organisational effectiveness. Beyond governance, serving as an NED is also an opportunity to give back to society, offering experienced professionals a meaningful way to apply their knowledge in service of the public good.

The table below provides an overview of the impact NEDs have across different sectors, highlighting the potential for individuals interested in public service to contribute meaningfully through these roles.

Sector	Role and Responsibilities of NEDs	Impact on the Organisation	Act of Service	Example
Government Services	Providing independent oversight and scrutiny of government agencies and public bodies.	Ensures transparency, accountability, and adherence to governance standards.	Contributing to public welfare by enhancing the effectiveness and efficiency of public services.	NEDs in the Ministry of Justice contribute to policy development and ensure the effective delivery of justice services.
	Advising on policy	Supports informed	Promoting the public	

Sector	Role and Responsibilities of NEDs	Impact on the Organisation	Act of Service	Example
	implementation and long-term strategic direction.	decision-making, leading to better policy outcomes and public trust.	interest by ensuring that the services provided meet the needs of citizens effectively.	
Healthcare	Offering guidance on clinical governance and patient safety in NHS trusts and healthcare boards.	Improves patient outcomes and enhances the quality of care by holding executives accountable.	Ensuring that healthcare services are patient-centred and of high quality, ultimately contributing to public health.	NHS England appoints NEDs to oversee NHS Trusts, ensuring they meet performance targets and maintain financial sustainability.
	Ensuring compliance with healthcare regulations and standards.	Builds public confidence in healthcare institutions, leading to better public health outcomes.	Upholding ethical standards in healthcare delivery, ensuring services are equitable and accessible to all.	
Education	Supporting the governance of schools, colleges, and universities through strategic oversight.	Enhances the quality of education and promotes the institution's mission and values.	Shaping the future by ensuring that educational institutions provide high-quality, inclusive education.	NEDs in Multi-Academy Trusts (MATs) ensure the delivery of high educational standards across schools, contributing to student outcomes and operational efficiency.
	Ensuring financial stewardship and effective use of resources in	Promotes sustainability and growth, ensuring educational	Helping to create environments where students can	

Sector	Role and Responsibilities of NEDs	Impact on the Organisation	Act of Service	Example
	educational institutions.	institutions can serve future generations.	thrive, contributing to society's long-term well-being.	
Financial Services	Overseeing risk management, regulatory compliance, and corporate governance in financial institutions.	Strengthens the financial stability and integrity of institutions, protecting the interests of stakeholders and the public.	Safeguarding public interest by ensuring that financial institutions operate responsibly and ethically.	Organisations such as Barclays and Lloyds Banking Group benefit from NEDs, who can oversee risk management practices, regulatory compliance, and ethical standards.
	Advising on strategic initiatives and long-term planning.	Contributes to sustainable growth and the responsible management of financial resources.	Promoting financial literacy and inclusion, ensuring that services are accessible to all segments of society.	
Charities/ Non-Profit	Providing strategic guidance and ensuring adherence to charitable objectives and regulatory standards.	Increases the charity's effectiveness in fulfilling its mission, benefiting the target communities.	Enhancing societal wellbeing by ensuring that charitable resources are used efficiently and for the intended purpose.	NEDs at organisations like the National Trust oversee the preservation of cultural heritage while ensuring sustainable financial management.
	Monitoring financial management and fundraising strategies.	Ensures the sustainability and growth of the charity, enabling it to	Supporting vulnerable and marginalised groups through	

Sector	Role and Responsibilities of NEDs	Impact on the Organisation	Act of Service	Example
		reach more beneficiaries.	effective charity governance.	
Retail	Contributing to governance, providing strategic guidance, ensuring compliance, and safeguarding the interests of shareholders.	NEDs provide an independent perspective on governance, ensuring compliance with regulations and ethical standards.	NEDs serve the public interest, protecting shareholders and the wider community.	NEDs at companies like Tesco provide oversight on sustainability initiatives and consumer engagement strategies, ensuring alignment with market trends and consumer demands.
	They help shape the company's Corporate Social Responsibility (CSR) initiatives, promoting sustainable and ethical practices.	Encourages the company to act responsibly towards society and the environment, benefiting the community.	NEDs can influence strategies that not only drive profit but also consider social responsibility, community engagement, and sustainability.	
Technology	Advising on innovation, digital transformation, and cybersecurity strategies.	Drives technological advancements and ensures the organisation remains competitive in a rapidly evolving sector.	Contributing to the ethical development and deployment of technology for societal good.	Companies like ARM Holdings and Ocado benefit from NEDs who can offer insights into regulatory compliance, cybersecurity, and strategic partnerships.
	Ensuring data privacy and compliance with digital regulations.	Protects consumer data and upholds the integrity of digital	Advocating for responsible innovation that considers the	

Sector	Role and Responsibilities of NEDs	Impact on the Organisation	Act of Service	Example
		services, boosting public trust.	broader societal impact of technology.	
Energy and Utilities	Providing oversight on sustainability, environmental impact, and regulatory compliance.	Enhances the organisation's reputation and ensures it meets its obligations to customers and the environment.	Ensuring that essential services like water, energy, and waste management are delivered reliably and sustainably.	NEDs at companies like National Grid oversee strategies for transitioning to renewable energy, ensuring the company's long-term sustainability and regulatory compliance.
	Advising on strategic planning and infrastructure development.	Supports long-term planning that meets the future needs of society, particularly in areas like renewable energy.	Promoting the adoption of green technologies and practices that contribute to environmental preservation and resilience.	

Why Serve as a Non-Executive Director (NED)

Serving as a Non-Executive Director (NED) is an opportunity to support an organisation's success and a powerful avenue for personal growth, leadership development, and broader societal impact. While NEDs provide independent oversight and strategic guidance, they also gain invaluable experience that enhances their own professional growth.

Becoming an NED allows individuals to refine their leadership and decision-making skills at the highest level. Boardroom discussions expose NEDs to complex challenges, requiring them to think critically, assess risks, and offer solutions that drive long-term success. This role provides a unique perspective on governance, finance, and corporate strategy, valuable skills that can be applied in various professional and civic roles.

Beyond influencing a single organisation, NEDs have the potential to drive industry-wide change. Many serve on regulatory or advisory boards, where their insights contribute to shaping policies and best practices. Whether in healthcare, education, housing, or corporate governance, NEDs play a vital role in ensuring ethical leadership and effective decision-making that benefits wider society.

For those passionate about making a difference, an NED role can be a gateway to further public service. Many leaders who start as NEDs go on to take positions in government, regulatory bodies, or larger charitable organisations. The role provides exposure to influential networks and a deeper understanding of how decisions at the highest levels impact communities, making it a natural progression for those looking to expand their influence.

Serving as an NED also opens doors to new professional relationships, connecting individuals with key decision-makers across industries. These networks can lead to further opportunities, collaborations, or mentorship roles. More importantly, it allows individuals to leave a legacy, ensuring that their experience and expertise contribute to meaningful, long-term improvements in the organisations and communities they serve.

Ultimately, serving as an NED is about more than just governance. It is a commitment to shaping better institutions, industries, and communities. Whether looking to give back, develop your expertise, or influence public policy, stepping into this role provides a platform to create lasting change.

Time Requirements

Many individuals pursue Non-Executive Director (NED) roles after stepping away from full-time executive positions, as these roles provide intellectual stimulation and a continued connection to their industry without the pressures of daily management. However, NED positions require a significant commitment. Responsibilities typically include attending board meetings, quarterly, monthly, or as needed, committee participation, strategic oversight, and advisory work. In addition, NEDs may be expected to engage with stakeholders, review key documents, and provide crisis support when necessary. The total time commitment varies depending on the organisation but ranges from 15 to 50 days per year. Some high-profile or complex roles may require even greater involvement, particularly during organisational change or governance challenges.

Compensation

Non-Executive Directors (NEDs) may receive compensation or allowances for their time and expertise, but the role is generally less financially lucrative than full-time executive positions. Compensation varies significantly depending on the organisation's size, sector, and financial standing. In large private corporations, NEDs can earn substantial fees, often ranging from £20,000 to over £100,000 per year, particularly in FTSE-listed companies. Public sector and NHS NED roles typically offer lower remuneration, usually between £5,000 and £25,000 annually.

In non-profit organisations, charities, and some public bodies, NEDs often serve voluntarily, motivated by a commitment to social impact rather than financial reward. Some charitable organisations reimburse travel and reasonable expenses, but no salary is offered. Regardless of the financial aspect, many NEDs find the role fulfilling, as it allows them to contribute their expertise to governance, strategy, and ethical oversight while supporting meaningful causes.

Skills and Qualities Required

Individuals aspiring to become Non-Executive Directors (NEDs) must possess a strong blend of skills and qualities to contribute to an organisation's governance effectively. Below are some of the essential qualities that enable NEDs to handle governance challenges and drive sustainable success. These qualities help ensure that they can provide strategic guidance while adhering to the principles of good corporate governance.

1. Independence:

NEDs must demonstrate the ability to think critically and make decisions free from bias or undue influence. This independence allows them to constructively challenge the executive team, ensuring that decisions are made in the best interest of the organisation and its stakeholders.

2. Experience:

Aspiring NEDs should have relevant professional experience in areas such as management, finance, law, or specific industry sectors. This expertise enables them to offer valuable insights in boardroom discussions and contribute with a deep understanding of the issues.

3. Integrity:

Integrity is a key quality for NEDs, as it underpins good governance. NEDs must maintain high ethical standards and always act honourably and transparently. This integrity reassures stakeholders that the board upholds the highest standards of conduct, building trust and confidence.

4. Sound Judgement:

Sound judgement is the ability to assess situations thoroughly and make informed decisions. NEDs need to carefully weigh various factors, considering both short-term and long-term implications and evaluating the potential risks and opportunities involved.

5. Commitment:

Commitment is essential for success in the NED role. NEDs must be dedicated to the organisation's mission and goals, demonstrating a willingness to devote the necessary time and effort. Their success depends on active involvement, thorough preparation, and a proactive approach, allowing them to make valuable contributions to the board's activities.

How to Become a Non-Executive Director (NED)

Becoming a Non-Executive Director (NED) requires a combination of leadership skills, industry experience, and a strong professional network. Aspiring NEDs should consider pursuing board-level training and familiarise themselves with corporate governance frameworks. Additionally, leveraging expertise in finance, legal, or operational roles can provide a competitive edge, making candidates more attractive to boards seeking strategic input.

Professional Development Programs

Various organisations and educational institutions offer specialised training programs for aspiring NEDs. Business schools, professional bodies like the Institute of Directors (IoD), and specialised training companies provide courses designed to equip individuals with the governance, financial acumen, and leadership skills required for NED roles. These programs also cover key areas such as risk management, boardroom dynamics, and regulatory compliance, which are crucial for those seeking a transition into an NED position.

Networking

Building a strong professional network is essential for aspiring NEDs. Attending industry-specific events and corporate governance conferences and joining organisations such as the Institute of Directors or the Financial Times Non-Executive Directors' Club can provide valuable opportunities to connect with experienced directors and decision-makers. Networking not only helps you stay informed about NED vacancies but also keeps you up to date with emerging trends in corporate governance.

Mentorship

Seeking guidance from experienced NEDs can be invaluable. A mentor can help you understand boardroom culture, assess your readiness for an NED role, and introduce you to relevant opportunities. Many aspiring NEDs find mentors through professional networks, executive search firms, or formal mentorship programs offered by industry bodies.

Volunteering

Voluntary roles on non-profit or charity boards are an excellent starting point for gaining board experience. These roles offer opportunities to develop governance skills, build a track record, and expand your professional network. Many successful NEDs began their journey by volunteering for such boards, which often value individuals passionate about their cause and eager to contribute.

Advertised Positions

NED roles are often advertised on specialised job boards such as NEDonBoard, Women on Boards, and the IoD's NED vacancy listings. Executive search firms like Spencer Stuart, Korn Ferry, and Odgers Berndtson also handle NED recruitment. The recruitment process typically involves submitting a detailed CV, participating in interviews with board members or shareholders, and undergoing assessments to ensure the candidate's suitability for the role. The focus is on a candidate's governance experience, strategic insight, and ability to contribute effectively to the board's decision-making processes.

Useful Resources for Aspiring Non-Executive Directors (NEDs)

Here are some platforms, directories, recruitment agencies, and organisations that offer information and opportunities for non-executive director positions.

Online Platforms and Directories:

Name	Description / What they offer
NEDonBoard	NEDonBoard is a professional body for non-executive directors in the UK. They offer a platform that connects aspiring and experienced non-executive directors with relevant opportunities. Their website provides resources, networking events, and a job board specifically for NED roles. https://www.nedonboard.com

Name	Description / What they offer
BoardEx	BoardEx is a comprehensive business intelligence platform that provides information on board-level executives. While it primarily focuses on executives, it also offers a directory of non-executive directors. The platform allows users to search for NED profiles based on various criteria. https://www.boardex.com
Nurole	Nurole is an online platform that connects highly qualified individuals, including non-executive directors, with board-level opportunities. They use a unique algorithm to match candidates with roles based on their skills and experience. Nurole also supports organisations in building diverse and inclusive boards. https://www.nurole.com
Exec-Appointments	Exec-Appointments is a platform that advertises executive-level roles, including non-executive director positions. It provides a search function and email alerts to notify candidates of relevant opportunities. https://www.exec-appointments.com
Boardmatch by Peridot	Boardmatch was launched to connect individuals with board-level positions in the charitable and non-profit sectors. Their online platform allows candidates to search for non-executive director roles in the third sector. https://www.peridotpartners.co.uk
NED Exchange	NED Exchange is an online platform connecting non-executive directors with organisations seeking their expertise. It offers a directory of NEDs and facilitates connections through its platform. https://www.nedexchange.co.uk
UK Business Angels Association (UKBAA)	UKBAA is an organisation that supports early-stage investors and connects them with high-potential growth businesses. While their main focus is angel investing, they occasionally advertise non-executive director opportunities on their website. https://ukbaa.org.uk
Women on Boards	Women on Boards is a platform dedicated to increasing gender diversity on boards. While their primary focus is on promoting women to board positions, they also provide opportunities for non-executive director roles. Their website offers resources, events, and a job board for NED positions. https://www.womenonboards.net

RECRUITMENT AGENCIES:

Name	Description / What they offer
Odgers Berndtson	Odgers Berndtson is an executive search firm that offers recruitment services for senior-level positions, including non-executive director roles. They have a dedicated board practice that specialises in board-level appointments. https://www.odgersberndtson.com
Russam	Russam is an executive recruitment agency that specialises in non-executive director appointments. They work with organisations across various sectors to identify and place suitable candidates in NED roles. https://www.russam.co.uk
Green Park	Green Park is an executive search and interim management firm that assists in non-executive director appointments. They have a team of experienced consultants who work closely with clients to understand their needs and find the right candidates for NED positions. https://www.green-park.co.uk
Perrett Laver	Perrett Laver is an international executive search firm that supports organisations in appointing non-executive directors. They have a dedicated team focused on board-level appointments and work across various sectors, including public, private, and non-profit. https://www.perrettlaver.com
Saxton Bampfylde	Saxton Bampfylde is an executive search and leadership consulting firm that assists in non-executive director recruitment. They have a dedicated team with expertise in board-level appointments and work with organisations across different industries. https://www.saxbam.com
Nolan Partners	Nolan Partners is a global executive search firm specialising in sports, media, and entertainment. While their primary focus is on these sectors, they also provide services for non-executive director appointments in related industries. https://www.nolanpartners.com
Nurole Board Search	In addition to their online platform, Nurole also offers a board search service. They use their extensive network and proprietary technology to identify and approach potential candidates for non-executive director roles.

Name	Description / What they offer
	https://www.nurole.com/board-search
Russell Reynolds Associates	Russell Reynolds Associates is a global leadership advisory and executive search firm. They have a board services practice that helps organisations recruit non-executive directors. https://www.russellreynolds.com/en/
Eton Bridge Partners	Eton Bridge Partners is an executive search and interim management firm. They have a dedicated board practice that assists with non-executive director appointments. https://etonbridgepartners.com
Heidrick & Struggles	Heidrick & Struggles is an executive search and leadership consulting firm. They have a board and CEO practice that supports organisations in recruiting non-executive directors. https://www.heidrick.com/en

Other Relevant Organisations:

Name	Description / What they offer
Institute of Directors (IoD)	The Institute of Directors is a professional membership organisation for directors and business leaders. While they don't offer a dedicated job board, they provide networking opportunities, events, and resources to help aspiring and current non-executive directors connect with relevant opportunities. https://www.iod.com
Financial Times Non-Executive Director Club	The Financial Times Non-Executive Director Club is an exclusive network for board directors and aspiring NEDs. While membership is required to access their services, they offer networking events, educational resources, and access to a community of experienced directors. https://www.bdp.ft.com/ned-club
The Non-Executive Directors' Association (NEDA)	The Non-Executive Directors' Association is a professional organisation that represents and supports non-executive directors across different sectors. They offer resources, events, and networking opportunities to enhance the skills and knowledge of NEDs. https://www.nedaglobal.com
The Financial Reporting Council (FRC)	The Financial Reporting Council is the UK's independent regulator responsible for promoting transparency and integrity in corporate governance and reporting. While not a job board, their website provides guidance, codes, and reports related to non-executive directors and corporate governance.

Name	Description / What they offer
	https://www.frc.org.uk
The Association of Independent Professionals and the Self-Employed (IPSE)	IPSE is a membership organisation that supports independent professionals and self-employed individuals. While they don't focus solely on non-executive directorships, they offer resources, events, and a platform to connect with potential opportunities. https://www.ipse.co.uk
Chartered Institute of Personnel and Development (CIPD)	CIPD is a professional body for HR and people development. They provide resources and networking opportunities that may be relevant for individuals seeking non-executive director roles. https://www.cipd.org/uk
Association of Corporate Treasurers (ACT)	ACT is a professional organisation for treasury professionals. Their main focus is treasury roles while occasionally advertising non-executive director opportunities relevant to their members. https://www.treasurers.org

Summary of Chapter 17
Non-Executive Directors

- **The Role of NEDs in Governance** – Non-Executive Directors (NEDs) provide independent oversight, strategic guidance, and ethical leadership across various sectors, ensuring transparency, accountability, and sound decision-making. The collapse of Carillion highlights the risks of ineffective governance when NEDs fail to challenge poor leadership decisions.
- **Impact Across Sectors** – NEDs play a critical role in diverse industries, including government services, healthcare, education, financial services, and charities. Their contributions range from policy guidance and financial oversight to ethical governance and risk management, directly affecting public trust and organisational success.
- **Personal and Professional Growth** – Serving as an NED enhances leadership and decision-making skills while offering opportunities for public service and industry-wide influence. Many NEDs leverage their experience to transition into regulatory, advisory, or government roles.
- **Time Commitment and Compensation** – NED roles require significant time investment, typically ranging from 15 to 50 days annually. Compensation varies widely, with high-profile private sector roles offering substantial remuneration, while many public and charitable sector NEDs serve voluntarily.
- **Pathway to Becoming an NED** – Aspiring NEDs should develop strong leadership skills, industry expertise, and governance knowledge. Training programs, professional networking, and mentorship are key avenues for securing board positions and making meaningful contributions to governance.

PART SIX

ACTS OF SERVICE BEYOND BORDERS

Chapter 18

Serving a Global Community

Not long ago, I concluded a mentoring session with someone thousands of miles away, someone I have never met in person, yet whose life I was able to impact through the power of connection. It amazes me how service is no longer confined to our immediate surroundings. With digital platforms, mentoring, inspiring, and serving transcends geography. The world has become smaller, and our influence can now extend to places we may never physically visit.

It is incredible how service is not limited to the local level; what once felt confined to my immediate community has expanded far beyond borders. Working in my neighbourhood, supporting schools, and stepping into public service roles were just the beginning. Over time, I realised that the same impact I had locally could be extended across cultures and continents.

As a certified life coach and mentor, I have had the privilege of guiding individuals seeking clarity, personal growth, and career development. Whether it's a young person in the UK struggling to find direction or a determined business owner in Africa working to turn their vision into reality, my mission remains the same: to inspire, equip, and empower people to thrive.

The Boundless Nature of Service

The power of service is no longer confined to physical presence. In the past, making an impact required being in the room, attending the event, or holding a formal role. Today, a single message, virtual session, or online initiative can transform someone's life, no matter where they are in the world.

While *The Act of Service* primarily focuses on roles and opportunities within the UK, leadership, mentorship, and civic engagement principles extend far beyond national borders. The ability to serve is not limited by geography. If you have knowledge, experience, or even a simple word of encouragement, you already have something valuable to offer. The key is to embrace the tools available and start where you are. You don't need a specific title or location to make a difference. Your willingness to uplift others is what truly matters.

True service is about who you can reach, not just where you live. Whether supporting someone next door or across continents, the impact you create has no borders. Even as this book highlights pathways to influence within the UK, the mindset and strategies shared can inspire action globally.

Extending Your Impact Beyond Local Community

Serving beyond your immediate environment is one of the most meaningful ways to contribute to global change. Whether addressing education inequality, supporting humanitarian efforts, or working towards sustainability, expanding your reach strengthens international collaboration, cultural exchange, and personal growth.

Engagement can take many forms. Some choose direct involvement abroad through humanitarian missions or development programs, while others provide remote support through mentorship, virtual volunteering, or fundraising for global causes. Regardless of the approach, both paths allow individuals to make a tangible difference in ways that align with their skills, values, and availability.

No matter your profession, background, or stage in life, the opportunity to serve is always within reach. The world has become smaller, and the potential for impact is greater than ever. The question is not where you serve but how far you are willing to let your service reach.

Participating Remotely

Remote service offers a meaningful way to support global causes without the need for travel. With flexible options that fit different schedules and skills, it enables more people to contribute to positive change from anywhere in the world. Here are some impactful ways to get involved:

- **Online Tutoring and Mentoring:** Help students from underserved communities worldwide by offering academic support or career guidance. Platforms like Teach For All connect volunteers with learners seeking educational advancement.
- **Digital Skill Sharing:** Use your expertise in areas such as coding, marketing, or graphic design to assist nonprofits and social enterprises. Websites like Catchafire match skilled volunteers with organisations needing technical support.
- **Virtual Fundraising:** Harness the power of social media and crowdfunding to raise awareness and financial support for global initiatives. Organisations like UNICEF and Doctors Without Borders welcome digital advocates to help expand their reach.
- **Translation and Transcription Services:** Multilingual volunteers can provide translation support for NGOs, helping them communicate with diverse audiences. Opportunities to assist with document translation and interview transcriptions are available through platforms such as Translators Without Borders.
- **Research and Content Development:** Contribute by conducting research, writing reports, or creating content for organisations tackling issues like climate change, human rights, and education. This is an excellent option for journalism, academia, or policy research professionals.

Physical Involvement Abroad

Traveling abroad to serve provides an enriching experience in different communities, offering a unique opportunity to make a direct, hands-on impact.

For those eager to engage with diverse cultures while contributing to global causes, here are some impactful ways to get involved:

- **Volunteering with NGOs and NonProfits:** Programs like Peace Corps, Habitat for Humanity, and international branches of the Red Cross enable volunteers to work on the ground in communities. This could involve building homes, improving healthcare systems, or supporting educational projects.
- **Teaching and Education:** Many countries with limited educational resources offer opportunities for volunteers to teach in schools. Programs such as Teach Abroad or United Nations Volunteers allow individuals to teach subjects like English, math, and science.
- **Medical Volunteering:** Healthcare professionals can provide critical medical support in underserved regions with limited access to healthcare. Organisations like Médecins Sans Frontières (Doctors Without Borders) or Project HOPE send volunteers to deliver essential medical care.
- **Conservation and Environmental Projects:** Volunteers passionate about environmental protection can contribute to global conservation efforts, including wildlife protection, reforestation, and marine conservation. Numerous programs across Africa, Asia, and South America, like Earthwatch or WWOOF (World Wide Opportunities on Organic Farms), focus on these vital initiatives.
- **Disaster Relief and Humanitarian Aid:** When natural disasters or humanitarian crises occur, international volunteers are often called upon for urgent relief efforts. Organisations like the International Rescue Committee (IRC) and CARE International deploy volunteers to provide hands-on support in affected regions.

Key Considerations for Serving Abroad

Engaging in global service through physical presence demands careful planning and consideration. Unlike remote participation, being physically present in another country requires a deeper commitment in terms of time, resources, and adaptability. From travel logistics to cultural nuances, several factors must be considered to ensure your contribution is meaningful and respectful. Below are important considerations for anyone thinking about serving abroad:

Qualifications and Skills

Global service opportunities require varying levels of expertise. Some roles, especially in fields like healthcare or education, may demand formal qualifications. For example, medical missions often need professionals like nurses or doctors, while educational projects may prioritise individuals with teaching experience. However, many organisations also welcome volunteers without specialised skills, offering on-site training to help them adapt and contribute effectively.

Cultural Awareness and Sensitivity

Serving in a foreign country means interacting with a culture that may differ significantly from your own. It's essential to understand local customs, social norms, and traditions to avoid unintentionally causing offence. Approach each experience with openness, adaptability, and respect for cultural differences. Doing so will enrich your experience and strengthen your relationship with the communities you serve.

Language Barriers

Language can present a significant challenge in global service work. While fluency in the local language may not always be required, having a basic understanding of key phrases can greatly enhance communication. Many organisations offer language training for volunteers, and platforms like Tandem or HelloTalk provide opportunities for language exchange. It's important to assess your comfort level with language barriers before committing to a placement.

Health and Safety

Ensuring your health and safety is a top priority when serving abroad. Different regions may have specific health risks, such as disease exposure or limited access to medical care. Prior to departure, make sure to receive any necessary vaccinations, research healthcare options in the destination country, and take preventive measures to protect your well-being. It's also essential to evaluate the political and social stability of the country you'll be travelling to.

Logistics and Travel Requirements

Travelling abroad for service requires careful logistical planning. You'll need to consider visa requirements, travel insurance, and accommodation arrangements. Some service programs assist with these details, while others may require you to manage them on your own. Understand the costs involved, including travel, lodging, and meals, and plan your budget accordingly.

Duration of Commitment

Consider how much time you can realistically commit to a global service project. Some programs are short-term, lasting only a few weeks or months, while others may require a longer commitment. Ensure that the duration of your service aligns with your personal and professional responsibilities at home.

Long-term Impact and Sustainability

Think about the long-term impact of your work. Ethical global service projects prioritise sustainability and aim to empower local communities in a way that ensures lasting benefits. Before committing to a project, evaluate whether it aligns with your values and contributes to a sustainable future for the communities involved.

Emotional and Mental Preparedness

Serving abroad, particularly in underprivileged or crisis-affected areas, can be emotionally challenging. You may encounter situations of poverty, suffering, or harsh living conditions, which can take a toll on your mental health. It's important to mentally prepare for these challenges and ensure you have a strong support system to help process your experiences.

Financial Considerations

Although many global service opportunities are volunteer-based, financial commitments may still be involved. Some organisations require volunteers to cover their own expenses, including travel, accommodation, and food. Others provide stipends or fundraising options to support volunteers. It's essential to understand the financial commitments beforehand and ensure you have the necessary resources or fundraising plans.

Alignment with Personal and Professional Goals

Participating in global service can be an immensely fulfilling experience, but it's also important to consider how the opportunity aligns with your long-term goals. Whether you are looking to gain new skills, experience a different culture, or contribute to a cause you are passionate about, reflect on how this opportunity fits within your broader personal or professional aspirations.

How to Find and Engage in Service Abroad

Engaging in international service is a meaningful way to make a positive impact while expanding your worldview. It provides opportunities for personal growth, cultural exchange, and a deeper understanding of global issues. By researching opportunities, assessing your skills, planning carefully, working with reputable organisations, and sharing your experiences, you can embark on a transformative journey that benefits both yourself and the communities you serve.

Below are key steps to discovering and participating in impactful service opportunities abroad:

Research and Identify Opportunities:

Begin by researching organisations, NGOs, and volunteer programs that align with your interests and values. Look for reputable organisations with a proven track record of positive impact. Online platforms and directories, such as those listed in the useful links section, can help connect you to international service opportunities.

Assess Your Skills and Interests:

Evaluate your strengths, expertise, and passions to determine how you can contribute meaningfully. For example:

- If you have a medical background, consider volunteering with healthcare organisations in underserved communities.
- If you're passionate about education, look for opportunities to support teaching programs in developing countries.
- If you have digital skills, explore remote volunteering options, such as supporting NGOs with technology, marketing, or administration.

Understanding what you can offer ensures that your contributions are both valuable and personally fulfilling.

Plan and Prepare:

Once you've identified a service opportunity, plan your engagement carefully. Consider logistical aspects such as travel, visas, accommodation, and necessary vaccinations. Familiarise yourself with local customs, social norms, and languages to ensure a respectful and enriching experience. The previous section on key considerations for serving abroad provides further guidance on these aspects.

Collaborate with Established Organisations:

Partnering with well-established organisations provides structure, support, and resources to ensure an impactful service experience. Choose organisations that prioritise sustainability and long-term community empowerment.

Working within existing frameworks increases the effectiveness of your contribution and helps ensure ethical engagement.

Fundraising and Financial Support:

International service often involves financial costs, including travel and living expenses. Explore ways to secure funding through:

- Crowdfunding platforms
- Grants and scholarships
- Support from friends, family, and local businesses

If travelling isn't feasible, you can still contribute by donating to reputable organisations working on causes that align with your values.

Reflect and Share Your Experience:

After completing your service, take time to reflect on your experiences. Document your journey through journaling, blogging, or social media to highlight the impact and encourage others to participate. Sharing your story can spark interest, raise awareness, and inspire more people to contribute to meaningful causes.

Useful Links for Global Service Opportunities

The following organisations offer valuable opportunities for individuals looking to make a global impact. You can explore their mission, programs, and ways to get involved through their websites.

Name	Description / What they offer
Amnesty International	Amnesty International provides opportunities for individuals to contribute to human rights campaigns, research, and advocacy efforts. https://www.amnesty.org.uk/
British Red Cross	The British Red Cross provides humanitarian assistance and support in the UK and internationally. They offer various volunteering opportunities, including emergency response, refugee services, health and social care, and more.

Name	Description / What they offer
	https://www.redcross.org.uk/
CARE International	A humanitarian organisation that focuses on global poverty reduction, humanitarian aid, and social justice. Volunteers can support emergency relief, development programs, and advocacy efforts. https://www.careinternational.org.uk
Catchafire	Catchafire connects skilled volunteers with non-profits, offering virtual and in-person volunteer opportunities across various areas of expertise. https://www.catchafire.org/
Conservation International	Conservation International focuses on biodiversity conservation and sustainable development to protect nature for the well-being of people. https://www.conservation.org/
Doctors Without Borders (Médecins Sans Frontières)	MSF is an international medical humanitarian organisation that provides emergency medical aid in countries affected by crises. https://www.doctorswithoutborders.org/
Earthwatch	Offers volunteer opportunities for individuals to engage in scientific research and environmental conservation through field projects worldwide. https://earthwatch.org
Engineers Without Borders UK	Engineers Without Borders UK offers volunteering and professional development opportunities for engineers to contribute to sustainable development projects worldwide. https://www.ewb-uk.org/
Global Greengrants Fund	Global Greengrants Fund provides funding and support to grassroots organisations around the world working on environmental and social justice issues. They offer opportunities for individuals to get involved in their grant-making process. https://greengrants.org
GlobalGiving	GlobalGiving is an online platform that connects donors with grassroots projects and organisations worldwide. They offer a range of volunteer and fundraising opportunities, allowing you to support projects aligned with your interests. https://www.globalgiving.org/
Greenpeace	Greenpeace is an international environmental organisation that campaigns for solutions to global environmental issues and advocates for peace and non-violence.

Name	Description / What they offer
	https://www.greenpeace.org.uk/
Habitat for Humanity International	Habitat for Humanity is a non-profit organisation that focuses on building homes and improving communities worldwide. https://www.habitat.org/
Idealist	A comprehensive database of volunteer and job opportunities worldwide. https://www.idealist.org
iEARN	iEARN is a global network that connects teachers and students to collaborate on projects focused on cross-cultural learning and making a positive impact. https://iearn.org/
International Rescue Committee (IRC)	The IRC responds to humanitarian crises worldwide, providing support to people affected by conflict and disaster. They have volunteer and employment opportunities in various fields, including health, education, and protection. https://www.rescue.org/
International Volunteer HQ (IVHQ)	IVHQ is one of the largest volunteer travel organisations, offering a wide range of projects in various countries. https://www.volunteerhq.org
Marine Conservation Society	The Marine Conservation Society is a UK-based charity that works to protect marine environments and promote sustainable seafood choices. https://www.mcsuk.org/
Mercy Ships	Mercy Ships operates hospital ships to provide free medical care to underserved communities around the world. https://www.mercyships.org.uk
Oxfam International	Oxfam is an international organisation dedicated to fighting poverty and injustice worldwide. They offer volunteering and internship opportunities in areas such as campaigning, fundraising, communications, and policy advocacy. https://www.oxfam.org/
Peace Corps	U.S. government-led volunteer program focusing on global development through education, health, agriculture, and community development. Available to UK citizens with dual U.S. citizenship. https://www.peacecorps.gov
Permaculture Association	Permaculture promotes sustainable and regenerative farming practices through education, training, and research.

Name	Description / What they offer
	https://permaculture.org.uk/
Projects Abroad	Projects Abroad is a global organisation offering volunteer programs in teaching, healthcare, conservation, and community development. https://www.projects-abroad.org
Project HOPE	Focuses on global health initiatives, including disaster relief, healthcare training, and capacity building. Opportunities exist for medical and non-medical volunteers. https://www.projecthope.org
Raleigh International	Raleigh International provides expeditions and volunteering opportunities focused on community development, environmental conservation, and youth empowerment. https://raleighinternational.org/
Red Cross and Red Crescent Societies	The International Federation of Red Cross and Red Crescent Societies (IFRC) is the world's largest humanitarian network, providing assistance during emergencies and supporting vulnerable communities. They offer volunteer programs and various ways to contribute to their work. https://www.ifrc.org
Restless Development	Restless Development engages young people in addressing development challenges through volunteer placements focused on education, health, and livelihoods. https://restlessdevelopment.org/
Save the Children UK	Save the Children provides opportunities in the UK and worldwide to support children's rights and well-being through volunteering, fundraising, and campaigning. https://www.savethechildren.org.uk/
Sea Shepherd Conservation Society	Sea Shepherd is an international marine conservation organisation that works to protect and preserve marine wildlife and habitats. https://seashepherd.org/
Taproot Foundation	Taproot Foundation mobilises skilled volunteers to provide pro bono services to non-profit organisations, furthering social change. https://taprootfoundation.org/
Teach for All	Teach for All is a global network of organisations that recruits and develops teachers to provide quality education in disadvantaged communities worldwide. https://teachforall.org/

Name	Description / What they offer
The United Nations High Commissioner for Refugees (UNHCR)	UNHCR works to protect and assist refugees and internally displaced persons worldwide. https://www.unhcr.org/uk/
United Nations Children's Fund (UNICEF)	UNICEF works to protect the rights and well-being of children worldwide. They offer volunteer opportunities, fundraising campaigns, and advocacy programs to support children in need. https://www.unicef.org
United Nations Volunteers (UNV)	UNV provides opportunities for individuals to volunteer abroad and contribute to global peace and development efforts. https://www.unv.org/
Voluntary Service Overseas (VSO)	VSO is an organisation that works to fight poverty and inequality through volunteer programs in developing countries. They offer a range of volunteer opportunities in sectors such as education, health, and livelihoods. https://www.vsointernational.org
Volunteer Action for Peace (VAP)	VAP offers international voluntary projects for individuals interested in promoting peace and intercultural understanding. They organise work camps, long-term volunteering, and youth exchanges worldwide. http://www.vap.org.uk
Volunteer World	Volunteer World provides a platform for international volunteering opportunities and how to apply. They connect volunteers with projects in over 70 countries. https://www.volunteerworld.com
World Food Programme	WFP is the leading humanitarian organisation fighting hunger worldwide. They offer opportunities to volunteer and support their mission of eradicating hunger and promoting food security. https://www.wfp.org
World Wide Opportunities on Organic Farms (WWOOF)	WWOOF connects volunteers with organic farms worldwide, allowing them to gain hands-on experience in sustainable agriculture. https://www.wwoof.org.uk/
World Wildlife Fund (WWF)	WWF is a leading conservation organisation that focuses on protecting the environment and endangered species. https://www.worldwildlife.org/

SUMMARY OF CHAPTER 18
SERVING A GLOBAL COMMUNITY

- **Service Beyond Borders**: Advancements in digital platforms allow individuals to mentor, inspire, and serve globally, breaking geographical limitations and extending impact beyond local communities.
- **Remote Engagement**: Online mentorship, digital skill-sharing, virtual fundraising, and research contributions offer accessible ways to participate in global service without physical travel.
- **Physical Involvement Abroad**: Opportunities such as NGO volunteering, teaching, medical missions, conservation efforts, and disaster relief provide hands-on experiences in international service.
- **Key Considerations for Global Service**: Factors like cultural awareness, language barriers, safety, financial planning, and long-term impact should be assessed before committing to international volunteering.
- **Finding and Engaging in Service Abroad**: Researching reputable organisations, aligning skills with opportunities, securing financial support, and reflecting on experiences help maximise the impact of global service initiatives.

About the Author

Bukky Okunade has dedicated her life to public service, embodying leadership, compassion, and an unwavering commitment to community empowerment. Her remarkable journey began in 1995 as a school governor, laying the foundation for decades of advocacy and transformative impact. Since then, she has held several influential roles, shaping policies and initiatives that have changed lives.

In 2002, Bukky was appointed an inner London magistrate, upholding justice with integrity and fairness. A year later, she co-founded a grassroots community organisation that evolved into a thriving community radio station, amplifying voices often unheard. Her public service continued as an elected councillor from 2006, where she championed policies to support social equity and youth development.

Bukky's pursuit of excellence is reflected in her academic and professional achievements, including earning a Master of Laws (LLM) degree from Birkbeck, University of London. With her legal acumen and leadership skills, she has served as a trusted mediator in complex community disputes and an inspiring life coach, guiding individuals towards personal and professional success.

Her dedication has earned her numerous accolades, recognising her outstanding societal contributions. Yet, she remains grounded in her mission to inspire and empower others through meaningful service.

A passionate mentor, Bukky has guided young people towards extraordinary achievements, from launching political careers to leading social change. Through TAG Radio, she has nurtured emerging talents, equipping them with the skills and confidence to thrive as future changemakers. Her work exemplifies her deep belief in the transformative power of mentorship and leadership.

In her book, *The Act of Service*, Bukky shares practical insights and heartfelt motivation for those aspiring to make a lasting impact. Her work stands as a testament to the power of service, inspiring individuals to lead with purpose and create meaningful change in their communities.

To learn more about Bukky Okunade, access valuable resources, and stay updated on her latest projects, visit her website:

www.bukkyofficial.com

Index

Printed in Great Britain
by Amazon

f707c318-d64c-4864-9f4c-2197ad989e85R01